FIVE MEDITATIONS
ON DEATH

Five Meditations on Death

In Other Words . . . On Life

FRANÇOIS CHENG

Translated by Jody Gladding

Inner Traditions

Rochester, Vermont • Toronto, Canada

Inner Traditions
One Park Street
Rochester, Vermont 05767
www.InnerTraditions.com

SUSTAINABLE FORESTRY INITIATIVE — Certified Sourcing
www.sfiprogram.org
SFI-00854

Text stock is SFI certified

Library of Congress Cataloging-in-Publication Data
Names: Cheng, François, 1929– author. | Gladding, Jody, 1955– translator.
Title: Five meditations on death : in other words . . . on life / François Cheng ; translated by Jody Gladding.
Other titles: Cinq méditations sur la mort. English
Description: Rochester, Vermont : Inner Traditions, 2016.
Identifiers: LCCN 2015049914 (print) | LCCN 2016009326 (e-book) | ISBN 9781620554944 (pbk.) | ISBN 9781620554951 (e-book)
Subjects: LCSH: Death. | Life.
Classification: LCC BD444 .C44513 2016 (print) | LCC BD444 (e-book) | DDC 128/.5—dc23
LC record available at http://lccn.loc.gov/2015049914

Printed and bound in the United States by Lake Book Manufacturing, Inc. The text stock is SFI certified. The Sustainable Forestry Initiative® program promotes sustainable forest management.

10 9 8 7 6 5 4 3 2 1

Text design by Virginia Scott Bowman and layout by Priscilla Baker
This book was typeset in Garamond Premier Pro

CONTENTS

PREFACE

BY JEAN MOUTTAPA

To communicate the essence of what he had to transmit on beauty—a theme that, to him, involved nothing less than the salvation of the world, as Dostoyevsky had once asserted—François Cheng felt the need to take a detour via orality, via the encounter with beings of flesh and blood. His five meditations on beauty in *The Way of Beauty* were thus shared with a group of friends over the course of five memorable evenings, before being shared with a wide audience through writing.

Seven years later, at the age of eighty-four, the poet felt almost an urgent need to speak of death. Or *in other words of life,* since his remarks, at the crossroads of Chinese and Western thought, are inspired by a passionate vision of "open life." And if he had found beauty too vital, too urgent a theme to make the subject of an academic treatise, what about death! That is why the same progression from oral exchange to writing was so clearly essential.*

Thus the present meditations too are born of sharing and marked by the seal of exchange between the poet and his interlocutors. Their readers will find themselves party to that exchange, they will be able to count themselves among the "dear friends" whom the author addresses. They will hear him, at the twilight of his life, truly express himself on a subject that many prefer to avoid. Here he is, baring his heart as perhaps he has never done before and delivering remarks both humble and daring. He does not claim to produce some "message" on the afterlife or to develop a dogmatic rhetoric; rather he attests to a vision.

A vision that ascends and reverses our perception of human existence, that invites us to contemplate life in the light of our own death—because to be conscious of death, according to Cheng, gives our fate its full meaning again, as an integral part of a great Adventure in becoming.

Thus, as in *The Way of Beauty*, here we are in a spiraling way of thought that does not hesitate to circle back to certain themes and words, to question them again more deeply. Nevertheless this way of thought is itself aware of the limits of language, because inevitably the moment arrives when death leaves us without a voice. Thus the need for silence . . . or the

---

*Like the sessions that gave rise to *Cinq méditations sur la beauté* (Paris, France: Albin Michel, 2006) [English edition: *The Way of Beauty: Five Meditations for Spiritual Transformation* (Rochester, Vt.: Inner Traditions, 2009)], those in question here also benefitted from the space of a beautiful yoga hall at the Center for the Fédération Nationale des Enseignant de Yoga. Warm thanks to those responsible, especially Ysé Tardan-Masquelier and Patrick Tomatis, for their hospitality.

poem, which is speech transfigured. That is why the fifth of these meditations assumes the poetic voice, so that beyond death, the song should have the last word.

JEAN MOUTTAPA is the director of the spiritualities imprint of Albin Michel. As a Christian, he is well-known for his commitment to interreligious dialogue, particularly through his involvement in the Aladdin Project and in actively organizing meetings between Jews and Muslims. He is the author of several books, including *Un Arabe face à Auschwitz* [An Arab Facing Auschwitz] and *Religions en dialogue* [Religions in Dialogue]. He also edited *A History of Jewish-Muslim Relations: From the Origins to the Present Day,* an important encyclopedia translated by Princeton University Press.

FIRST MEDITATION

Dear friends, thank you for coming, thank you for filling this welcoming space with your presences. At this previously arranged hour, between day and night, we have gathered together. And beginning from this moment, the language that we share is going to weave a golden thread about us and try to give rise to a truth that can be shared by all.

Nonetheless, if we think about it, we must admit that we come from afar. Each of us is heir to a long lineage, made up of generations we do not know, and each of us has been determined by inextricable blood ties that we did not choose. Nothing necessitates our desire and ability to be here together, to find some meaning in the simple fact of being together in this place. Isn't it true that we are lost in the depths of an enigmatic universe where, according to many, pure chance rules? Why is the universe here? We do not know. Why is life here? We do not know. Why are we here? We know nothing, or almost nothing. Once again, according to many, it was by chance that the universe came about one day. At the beginning something extremely dense exploded into billions and billions of shards. Much later it was by chance that on one of those shards life one day appeared. Improbable encounter of a few chemical elements and voilà, it took! Once the process was set in motion, "it" did not stop growing, increasing in volume and complexity, transmitting and transforming itself until the advent of the beings that we call "humans." What significance do humans have in relationship to the gigantic, that is to say, limitless, existence of the universe? Is the shard on which life appeared greater than a grain of sand in the midst of countless other shards? According to a widely held view, humans will one day be obliterated, life itself will be obliterated, leaving no more trace than a dry crust, without the universe even realizing it. From this perspective isn't it a little pathetic, even completely ridiculous, for us to take ourselves seriously, for us to gather here this evening and propose to meditate in a scholarly fashion upon death, and therefore upon life?

But how to deny that, if we are here, it is because this questioning exists and impels us? That it exists is already in itself an indication. If there were absolutely no possible meaning to our existence, the very idea of meaning would never have occurred to us. Whereas we know that humanity has forever pondered the reason for its presence within the universe, this universe it has learned to know a little and to love a lot. We also know that this questioning is all the more fraught because at the same time we know we are mortal. Never letting up, death drives us into our final corner. That is undoubtedly why I have the temerity to present myself before you. I have no particular qualifications for this. A few traits, incredibly banal overall, constitute my identity: I ought to have died young, and I ended up living quite a long time; I spent much time, let us say all my time, reading and writing and above all thinking and meditating; I partake of two cultures located at the two poles of the vast Eurasian continent, different enough to literally tear me apart and to enrich me as well if I can only limit myself to the best parts of both. My words will be marked by this confrontation of a lifetime.

Let me say now, straight out, that I number among those who locate themselves resolutely in the order of life. For us, life is in no way an epiphenomenon within the extraordinary adventure of the universe. We do not accept the view according to which the universe, being only matter, would have created itself without knowing it, unaware of its own existence from start to finish for those billions of years. In total ignorance of itself, it was supposedly capable of engendering conscious, active beings who, in the space of an infinitesimal time lapse, supposedly saw it, knew it, and loved it, before soon disappearing. As if all that had been for nothing . . . No indeed, we flatly deny this nihilism that has become commonplace today. Of course we grant matter its full value, without which nothing would exist. We also observe its slow evolution and its awakening to life. But for us, from the beginning, the principle of life is contained in the advent of the universe. And the mind, which bears this principle, is not a simple derivative of matter. It partakes of the Origin, and thus of the whole process of the appearance of life, which strikes us with its astounding complexity. Aware of the tragic conditions of our fate, we nevertheless allow life to overwhelm us with all its fathomless depths, its flood of unknown promises, and its indescribable springs of emotion.

I personally have an additional reason for being among those advocates of life: I came from what used to be called the "third world." We then formed the tribe of the damned, the eternally broken in body and spirit, bearers of suffering and grief, in such a state of ruin that the least crumb of life was received by us as an unhoped-for gift. As the have-nots we had some motive for vowing infinite love for life: because we had drunk all the bitter dregs of existence, we had also, from time to time, tasted unheard-of delights.

Thus we, the others, who reject any form of nihilism, acknowledge that we say yes to the order of life. Whatever our education and our convictions, that is where we return in some way to the intuition of the Tao. The Way, that gigantic directed march of the living universe, shows us that a Breath of life, beginning from Nothing, made Everything come about. Like the materialist for whom "there is nothing," we also speak of Nothing, but this Nothing signifies Everything. That is why, adopting the expression of Lao Tzu, the father of Taoism, we can say that "what is comes from what is not, and what is not contains what is."

There we have a mystery that seems to surpass our understanding. Maybe not completely, because on our very modest scale we have a fairly intimate experience of Nothing, by the very fact that we are mortals. Death lets us see for ourselves the incredible process by which Everything topples over into the Nothing. Over the course of our lives, each of us has been confronted up close or at a distance with the deaths of those dear or unknown to us, and on another level, we have "died" many times ourselves. That is what makes us aware of the omnipresence and power of death—individual death and death of the species. But curiously, here again, an intuition also tells us that it is our consciousness of death that makes us see life as an absolute good and the advent of life as a unique adventure that nothing could replace.

However, before being able to advance one step, our meditation nevertheless hits up against the enigma of death itself, a double enigma: on the one hand, we are not in a position to comprehend the reality of death—no one has ever come back from beyond the fateful boundary to bear witness; on the other hand, neither have we the capacity to imagine concretely an order of life in which death would not exist. We all hope for life to last an eternity, and that hope is wholly legitimate: caught up in an adventure so full of ordeals, we are entitled to aspire to it. But are we really in a position to enjoy an accurate vision of what is called "eternal life"? Do we know by and according to what conditions such an order of life is conceivable? To have even the slightest idea of it would undoubtedly require a far more daring, more arduous effort of the imagination. We will return to it in our last meditation.

For the time being, let us nevertheless try for a moment to imagine, according to our experience of life here, a form of existence in which beings would be totally unaware of death. Thus they would be there forever, contemporaries forever. Moreover, words like *forever* and *contemporary* probably would not exist in their vocabulary, since time, de facto, would be absent from their universe. Everything having been given forever, they would have no idea of dispersal and renewal, much less of transformation or transfiguration. Everything being repeatable and deferrable, they would have no irresistible impulse or irrepressible desire for fulfillment.

They would feel no astonishment, no gratitude with regard to existence, perceived by them as a given that would continue indefinitely and never as an unhoped-for, irreplaceable gift.

Let us go no further in the description of this hypothetical world. Already it has the merit of making us aware of what constitutes the essence of life. A word comes to mind that seems to characterize this notion, the word *becoming*. Yes, that's it, *life:* something that comes about and that becomes. Once it comes about, it enters into the process of becoming. Without becoming, there would be no life; life is life only in becoming. From there we can understand the importance of time. It is in time that this unfolds. As for time, it is precisely the existence of death that has conferred it on us! Life-time-death is an indissociable whole, unless it is rather death-time-life. We can juggle them as we like, but we cannot escape these three concomitant, complicit entities that determine all living phenomena. Because if time seems to us a terrible devourer of lives, it is at the same time the great provider of them. We suffer its hold; that is the price we pay for entering into the process of becoming. That hold is manifest in the unceasing cycles of births and deaths; it establishes the tragic condition of our fate, a condition that could also be the grounds for a certain grandeur.

The bodily death that is the cause of our anguish and our terror, that in the hands of criminals becomes the supreme instrument of Evil—a theme to which we will devote another meditation—we discover with alarm is thus necessary to life. We discover this either with alarm or with reverence, according to our perspective, because death can prove to be the most intimate, most secret, and most personal dimension of our existence. It can be that crux of necessity around which life is articulated. In this sense, Francis of Assisi's *Canticle of the Creatures* is revolutionary for calling bodily death "our sister." We are thus offered a change in perspective: instead of staring at death in horror from this side of life, perhaps we can integrate death into our vision and imagine life from the other side, from our death. From that position, while we are alive, our orientation and our actions would always be surging toward life.

Without this reversal, we remain dominated by a closed view according to which, no matter what we do, our life fizzles out with a conclusion that is summed up in one word: nothingness. It follows that we see the unfolding of our life as the prison sentence of one condemned to death, whose execution is deferred but inescapable, or as the course of a car driven by a maniac at breakneck speed until the accident happens, both unforeseen and foreseeable. On the other hand, viewing life beginning from a deep understanding of our death, we enjoy a more open vision to the extent that, exactly in accordance with the process of the origin of life, we are taking part in the great Adventure, and each moment of our life is thus a surge toward life.

Here our meditation arrives at a turning point. To help us move forward, let us listen to those among our predecessors who seriously confronted the question of death. Following Heidegger's example, beyond philosophical speculation, let us trust the words of poets, not for their lyricism, but for the flashes of intuition that have inspired them, for their eminently embodied words. Let us think of Ovid, Dante, the English metaphysical poets, Milton, and Eliot, and on the French side poets like Lamartine, Baudelaire, Péguy, Valéry, and Claudel. But the most original perspective is indisputably

Rilke's. From his famous early poem "O Lord, Give Us Each Our Own Death" to his final work, the *Duino Elegies,* death was his life's central theme. I suggest that we allow ourselves a little time to listen to his voice. I would be remiss not to do this, because I am so fundamentally in accord with him, which became clear to me the first time I read the words "O Lord, give us each our own death."

It was not long after my arrival in France at the end of 1948; I was almost twenty years old. I felt such resonance with this poem that I believed I could hear in it my own voice. Let me point out that prior to that time, all the years of my youth and adolescence in China had been dominated by war: the war of resistance against the Japanese (1937–1945) and the civil war beginning in 1946. Full of unrest, China had sunk into wretchedness. Against the backdrop of fighting, exile, bombing, diseases with names synonymous with death—tuberculosis, malaria, meningitis, cholera . . . —our lives hung for years by barely a thread. Those in my generation thought we would die young—me more than others because of my fragile health. Nevertheless our desire to live had never been so intense. Our hunger and thirst for existence were without bounds. The slightest ray of sunshine, the smallest drop of dew made our hearts pound; the least sip of soymilk or mouthful of wild fruit were infinite delicacies to us; the passion of love already had us in its grip, we burned with it, the taste of honey and ashes.

Later, my first poem in French, a quatrain, echoed this experience:

> *We have drunk so much dew*
> *In exchange for our blood*

That the earth, burnt a hundred times,
Is very grateful to us for being alive.

Early on, then, I was aware that it was death's proximity that drove us in our passionate urgency to live, and that above all, death was within us like a lover who was drawing us toward a form of realization. That is how it works within a fruit tree that passes irresistibly from the stage of leaves and blossoms to the one of fruits—fruits that signify both a state of full being and consent to the end, to their fall to the ground. Having begun writing at the age of fifteen, my form of realization was poetry. I repeated to myself, "It doesn't matter how long my life lasts, as long as I die a death that is my own, as long as I die a poet." To die a poet, like Keats, like Shelley, whose portraits decorated my room.

Now let us read Rilke's poem, from book III of his *Book of Hours,* "The Book of Poverty and Death":

O Lord, give us each our own death
Which is truly born of this life,
Where we found love, meaning, and our
    distress.

Because we are only leaves and bark,
The great death that each of us carries
    within,
Is that fruit around which everything turns.

And for that fruit maidens one day
Rise like a tree that springs from a lute,
And boys dream of becoming men,

And adolescents confide in women
Their anguish that no one else understands.
It is in this fruit that all things seen
Remain eternal, even those long gone by
And all those who created and built
    enveloped it
With a universe, froze it, melted it,
Irrigated it with wind and light.
In it, all heat was absorbed:
The heart and the white passion of the brain . . .

But your angels, Lord, like clouds of birds
Pass over; they find all these fruits still
    *green.**

Rilke expresses the passionate wish that the death of each of us be a death that belongs to us, because it is born of us like fruit. And he does not fail to notice, as we all have, that if the fruit falls to the ground, it finds itself close to the roots again; fertilizing the soil, it takes part in their regenerative power. Let us recall here that in Chinese, fruit is called "*kuo-tzu,*" which means an envelope containing the essence and the seeds. It signifies both a form of achievement and the possibility of rebirth in a different form. The roots are simultane-

---

*The quotations from R. M. Rilke follow the translation of my friend Maurice Betz, sometimes adapted here by the author, in *Poésie* [Poetry] (Paris, France: Émile-Paul Frères, 1938). Additionally, the English translation used Susan Ranson's and Annemarie Kidder's translations as references: *Rainer Maria Rilke's The Book of Hours* (Rochester, N.Y.: Camden House, 2008); and *Book of Hours: Prayers to a Lowly God* (Evanston, Ill.: Northwestern University Press, 2002), respectively.

ously the place of death and of birth. Thus in other poems he advises us to stay close to where the roots are; that is where our own death will take place.

This advice is not in the least inspired by a feeling of fatality. To reunite with one's own death in advance is to reunite with the source of life. It is to reunite with the far off Origin where the unbelievable adventure began, which, starting from Nothing, made Everything happen.

In Rilke, this is the beginning of a reversal in perspective, the very one that we described earlier: instead of staring at death from this side of life, imagining life from the position of death.

Rilke would subsequently expand his vision. But already we can notice a singular coincidence: the poet's intuition corresponds closely to the great lesson that Lao Tzu offers in the *Tao Te Ching*. In chapter 25, Lao Tzu asserts that the Way's course is circular:

> *Such is the mother of the universe.*
> *As it lacks a name, I call it the Way,*
> *Lacking other words, I call it great.*
> *Greatness means extensive,*
> *Extensive means distance,*
> *To go far away and to return again.*

And in chapter 40 we can read:

> *Return, the movement of the Way,*
> *Weakness, the law of its use,*
> *All things are born of what is,*
> *What is of what is not.*

Later, Taoist thought compares the Way to a river. Before flowing into the sea, the river seems to follow an irreversible course, fruitlessly. In reality, as it flows, some of its water evaporates and rises into the sky. There it is transformed into clouds, to fall later in the mountains as rain, which will replenish the river at its source. That is the fundamental law of how life functions, which the Chinese poetic and pictorial tradition revealed long before the recent development of ecological science.

Lao Tzu invites us to follow the example of the Way's circular course that continually returns to the Origin to replenish itself: each of us similarly can make an "early return" in our own lives.* This means precisely the return to the roots, the return to the Origin where the source of the truly Everlasting is found. We cannot help but think of these lines by Rilke:

> *Anticipate all farewells as if they were behind*
> *you, like the winter that is just passing.*
> *Because among the winters there is one so*
> *long that in wintering over your heart*
> *will have surmounted everything.*

Rilke was not familiar with Taoism. As a German language poet, he was primarily influenced by the great figures of Germanic poetry: Goethe, Hölderlin, Novalis, Heine, and so on. It happens that in the height of Romanticism, Goethe and Hölderlin had both known the experience of death through passionate love. We know that Goethe wrote *The Sorrows of Young Werther* at the end of an extremely unhappy love affair. After reading this book, many young men, driven to despair

---

*Tao Te Ching, chapters 16, 28, 33, 52, 59.

by love as well, committed suicide. Goethe himself had been saved by his writing.

From then on, throughout his life, he never forgot the injunction that he had issued to himself even as he had proposed it to the world: "Die and become!" As for Hölderin, he nurtured an absolute but impossible passion for Suzette Gontard, a married woman. She died of it; he fell into a kind of madness even as he continued to compose short poems that gradually grew calmer. Previously in his great plays, he had expressed his aspiration for the Open. Rilke took these two notions—"die and become" and "aim toward the Open"— and made them his own, which would allow him to expand his overall vision of life and death.

The Open, from Hölderlin's perspective, refers to the state of being or infinite space that certainly contains death but is not hindered or constrained by the awareness of death. Rilke translates it more concretely with the notion of the "Double Realm" that unites the two sides of life and of death, and he invites us to locate ourselves within its depths, rather than clinging to one side or the other. In the first of the *Duino Elegies* he asserts:

> *But the living make the mistake of*
> *distinguishing too sharply.*
> *The angels, it seems, do not always know if*
> *they are moving*
> *Among the living or the dead.*
> *The eternal current carries along all the ages*
> *of man, through*
> *The two realms, and in both of them*
> *Its great roar rises over their voices.*

In one of the *Sonnets to Orpheus,* written at the same time as the *Elegies,* he confirms:

> *Only the one who has raised his lyre*
> *Already among the shades*
> *Can have prescience and can proclaim*
> *Infinite praise.*
>
> *Only the one who has eaten poppies*
> *With the dead, their poppies,*
> *Will never again forget*
> *The softest tone.*
>
> *The reflection in the pool often*
> *Becomes blurred for us:*
> *Know the true Image.*
>
> *In the Double Realm alone*
> *Will the voices become*
> *Eternal and tender.*

With regard to the Open, Rilke remarks moreover that humans have to learn from the animals. Because when animals open their eyes, they see the Open, and when they run, they go toward pure, limitless space, whereas humans, from childhood on, are brought up to focus on only the tangible world, supposedly secure and thus carefully enclosed. The shadow of death is evicted from this closed world, although without successfully banishing the idea of an end, conceived as ruin or wreck, an end that comes closer each day. Doesn't

Heidegger say, "As soon as a man is born, he is old enough to die"? In Rilke's eighth elegy we read:

> *What is beyond we can only know*
> *By looking at an animal; because from*
> * childhood on*
> *We are turned and made to look back*
> *At the world of forms, not toward the Open*
> *Which, in the eyes of an animal is so deep,*
> *Free of death. We human are the ones who see*
> * death.*
> *The free animal always has its demise*
> * behind it;*
> *Ahead of it, God. When it moves forward,*
> * it moves*
> *Toward the eternal, as a spring flows.*

The poet never forgot his vivid memory of a spring evening in Russia evoked in his *Sonnets to Orpheus* (I, 20): a white horse that had come from the village to spend the night in the meadow was galloping completely free, and along its neck its mane rippled to the pulse of its blood, which resonated with the rippling waves that animate the universe. Once again, that scene seems to us close to the Taoist vision. Moreover it reminds us of two famous lines by Tu Fu addressed to a steed of Ferghana:

> *There where you go, no limit,*
> *To you may be entrusted death and life!*

Dear friends, we have reached the hour that announces night, that moment when the day ends, when another day arises. We feel the enlivening current of time passing: we submit to it, we consent to it. Thus let us accept the reversal of our position, and with it our perspective. Let us agree not to attach ourselves only to the side of life, but to locate ourselves in the depths of the Double Realm, where we will enjoy a more comprehensive view of our personal becoming within the universal becoming. There, in the course of the ceaseless progress of the Way that proceeds from Nothing toward Everything, from Non-Being toward Being, we too, from our profoundest depths, can follow the process that goes from death to life— and not from life to death—with a view to the fruit of the soul that will absorb pain and joy, tears and blood.

I do not want to fail to point out that the depths of the Double Realm is the ideal space for dialogue between the living and the dead. Let us be clear that this is not a matter of delighting in the universe of the dead. The dialogue in question simply involves beings who lived like us, who bear within every hunger and thirst, a whole world of unachieved desires, and who experience another state of life. Thus at the heart of the Double Realm, the dead are not, as is so often the case today, those transported like the nameless dying to some corner of the hospital and then, once dead, to some corner of the morgue, and finally to a box of ashes after cremation—those we avoid thinking about too much. On the contrary, here their murmurings reach us, infinitely moving and illuminating, murmurs that well up from the heart, words close to the essence, as though filtered by the great test. Because with the dead we gain by remaining all ears: they have much to say to us. Having undergone the great test, they are in some ways the initiated. They are in a position to rethink and relive life differently, to measure life by the yardstick of eternity. They can watch over us like so many guardian angels. Provided that we are not so ungrateful as to stash them among the forgotten, they can do something for us. Yes, in their way, they can protect us. This perspective can also help us to overcome our grief when we are in mourning.

If I express myself in this way, it is also because I come from a country that cultivated the worship of ancestors for thousands of years—even if this practice is fast disappearing today in China. For each family and village, the temple retained a register where the names of the ancestors were inscribed, and one learned to venerate them. In many houses altars were erected dedicated to them. On the Day of the Dead, many generations gathered around tombs, where each family member, bowing low, made the gesture of sweeping. A meal might also have been eaten together there, in an atmosphere of trusting, peaceful communion.

Patient, poignant human lineage! Going back so far, yet still not lost in the mists of time, in a trail of smoke: it is concrete, it is alive. Our impression of a countless anonymous crowd behind us fading into the fog of the past is a false one. Because in reality, we count only three or four generations per century and thirty or forty per millennium—that's relatively few, so our ancestors are much closer to us than we think. Here lies a transmission of hopes and promises that requires our respect and that, to a certain degree, gives value and meaning to our fate.

To remember the dead is thus, in a more universal sense, to learn gratitude toward them and, through them, toward life. Since our infancy, haven't we benefitted from the care and kindness of an undreamt-of number of individuals who have kept us alive: our parents certainly, and other close relatives, and beyond the family, friends, doctors, and those unknown to us whose actions have guarded us from danger. Many of them are no longer in this world. If we can extend our consideration further, we would also think more often of all the soldiers who have sacrificed themselves during wars, of all the rescuers who have given their lives during catastrophes, of all the experts in various fields who have allowed humans to live better and longer. Humanity rediscovers itself in each individual and each individual who embraces life takes part in the adventure of humanity, which is an integral part of a much greater adventure: that of the living universe coming into being.

What potential Open is there for humanity and for each of us? A legitimate question, which we are certainly not in a position to answer definitively. It is nonetheless permissible to speak of it, which we will do in our final meditation.

To summarize everything we have been able to propose thus far, let us repeat: to incorporate death into our vision is to receive life as a priceless gift of generosity. "Death," wrote Pierre Teilhard de Chardin, "is charged with practicing, at the very depths of ourselves, the opening we desire." Conversely, to close our eyes to death by barricading ourselves in against it is to reduce life to a miserly savings from which we would dole out our expenditures coin by coin, one day to the next.

In conclusion, let us listen to the great voice of Etty Hillesum who was gassed by the Nazis in Auschwitz. Beforehand, already threatened but still fully alive, she noted one day in her journal: "By saying that I have settled my accounts with life I mean that the eventuality of death is integrated into my life; because to look death in the face and accept it as an integral part of life is to enlarge that life. Conversely, from now on to sacrifice a bit of this life to death, out of fear and refusal to accept death, is the best way to safeguard only a poor little end of a crippled life, hardly deserving to be called life. That seems like a paradox: by excluding death from our life, we deprive ourselves of a complete life, and by welcoming it, we enlarge and enrich our life."*

*Une vie bouleversée [A Life Turned Upside Down] (Paris, France: Seuil, 1985).

SECOND MEDITATION

Dear friends, once more we are here together because we are preoccupied with a theme we have in common, this theme of death, from which no one can hide. Last time I proposed reversing our perspective. Instead of staring at death from this side of life, we could view life from our death, conceived not as an absurd end but as the fruit of our being. Because in an uncertain world fraught with the unpredictable, we possess only one absolute certainty: each of us must one day die.

Nevertheless, have we nothing more to say regarding this absolute? I think we do, for the simple reason that, because of life, death does not absolutely seem to us an absolute. In reality, if life did not exist, there would be no death. As death is the cessation of a certain state of life, its "absolute" cannot be born of itself. It can only be imposed by another even greater absolute, if I may say so, namely the one by which life comes about. This Origin has imposed death as one of its own laws and therefore death itself has become one proof of the absolute nature of life. We cannot think of life without thinking of death, any more than we can think of death without thinking of life. But within that indivisible binomial, it is life that has preeminence. Will death have the last word? Nothing could be less certain.

Let us clarify something right now, even if it means coming back to expand upon it later in the course of our meditations: the absolute nature of life means that, offering itself as a gift to each of us, it is also a requirement. It implies a certain number of fundamental laws that guarantee an open life and therefore true freedom. To live is not limited to the fact of bodily existence. To live involves the entire being, composed of a body, a mind, and a soul. Moreover, to live engages the individual being in the adventure of Being itself. Each of us is linked to others, and all of us are linked to an immense Promise that since the Origin has ensured the course of the Way. In this basic linkage that is borne out on all levels there is something like a pact, an alliance implying tacit responsibilities between each destiny and what rules over the destiny of the universe. To designate what is allotted to each life, Chinese thought proposed the notion of the "mandate of Heaven." Each of us has a duty to see that mandate through to the end without artificially interrupting it. It is precisely in confronting the trials of that "end" that each being becomes aware of its irreducible truth, its irreplaceable role. That is why suicide, whatever may be said of it, is generally perceived as a tragedy in relation to Being, a kind of failure.

Life has preeminence, as I have said. But that does nothing to diminish the fact that we are in a predicament. On Earth we humans are caught in an implacable snare: the certainty of death without knowing either its day or hour becomes the source of all uncertainties. Despite our thousand measures aimed at reassuring ourselves, we live under the threat of disease, accidents, fatal conflicts, the loss of loved ones. The result of which is permanent anguish. Given this situation, there is indeed a place for speaking of the miracle of being here together, sharing that rare happiness of a true exchange.

I just uttered the words *miracle* and *happiness*. It is certainly not an exaggeration to pair these two terms: happiness seems miraculous to us because it is neither frequent nor, most importantly, long lasting. Our awareness of the death of all things makes it so that our most luminous moments of happiness are always veiled in regret. Each of us can confirm this point with our own personal memories. Rather than delving into my own, I will simply recall a scene related by François Mauriac.

The academician paid a visit one day to his colleague Maurice Genovoix. As permanent secretary of the Academy, Genovoix's residence was in the Palais Mazarin. The apartment that comes with this position opens onto the Seine and offers one of the most beautiful views of Paris: at the center is moored the Pont des Arts, like a barge laden with ancient dreams, and off to its right, the Vert-Galant leading the glorious architectural procession of Notre-Dame and the Conciergerie, while on the other bank sprawls the Louvre with its rhythmic magnificence defying the centuries. On this spring evening, the pink light of the setting sun merging with the water of the river united sky and earth into a whole as sweet and light as the gulls flying about here and there or the clouds drifting in the distance, unconcerned. The two men, already well along in years, stood there quietly overcome with feeling, until Genevoix let out a sigh, "And to think that we must leave all this!" A melancholy phrase that serves to remind us that no happiness is indefinitely repeatable, that every happiness is a miracle. That said, the fact no less remains that the promise of happiness constitutes the sunlit slope of life. Despite the many misfortunes that life has in store for us, it nevertheless offers a potential number of happinesses great and small, so much so that a positive thinker might claim that in fact life is peppered with miracles—not even taking into account that it itself is a miraculous occurrence. Hence this enormous paradox: the awareness of death that impales us is far from being a purely negative force. It makes us see life no longer as a simple given but really as an unbelievable, sacred gift. It inspires in us a sense of value by transforming our lives into so many unique entities. Malraux's elegant turn of phrase comes to mind: "A life is worth nothing, but nothing is worth a life."

The uniqueness of each life: this is an idea that moves us up a notch in our understanding of the human adventure. This uniqueness is not limited to the human body alone; it is evident throughout nature: not one leaf is like another leaf, not one butterfly the same as another butterfly. Among humans, the uniqueness in question also involves all the work of the mind and all the awakening of the soul. It is each entire being who is unique and who, against the backdrop of death, creates his or her own singular destiny. "Death transforms life into destiny," Malraux again so aptly said. Thus it follows that the universe is not simply a jumble of entities acting blindly upon one another. It is formed by an extraordinary multiplicity of beings, each of which, moved by the desire to live, follows a directed trajectory, a trajectory that is absolutely his or her own. An irresistible power makes it urgent for us to move forward. And we know that power is nothing other than irreversible time.

Time truly is the great organizer that sweeps all living beings along in the awesome process of becoming. At the heart of the process, we humans, the only beings conscious of being mortal, find ourselves in a very peculiar situation. Each of us at one time or another in our existence comes to understand that our uniqueness itself is both a privilege and a limitation. We become aware that time is not granted to us indefinitely, that the limited time allotted to us makes it urgent for us to live fully. Doesn't this way of thinking threaten to trap the individual in a frightening stance of pride and self-importance? This threat is very real; it is one of the sources of evil. We will have an opportunity to come back to this point in another meditation. For the moment let us note what simple good sense teaches us: if I am unique, then others are unique as well, and the more unique they are, the more unique I am. And all the more so because my uniqueness can only be proven and experienced through confronting or communing with that of others. This is where the possibility of saying "I" and "you" begins, where language and thought begin—and this is confirmed most intensely by the bonds of love. Thus, beyond all the inevitable antagonisms, it exists as a fundamental solidarity that is established between the living. Eventually we come to understand that the happiness we seek always results from an encounter, an exchange, a sharing.

In the light of what we just said, our gathering here this evening stands out as unusual. If the enigma of death pushed us into coming, it is because each of us bears a history full of dreams and quests, trials and suffering, questions and hope. Each of us wants to compare our experience to that of others, convinced that a life truth will arise from what the Chinese call the breath of the median Void, the breath created by an authentic intersubjectivity. And nevertheless we know that in seeking this life truth, we cannot expect a simple answer, formulated as a dry theorem, since we recognize that it is not only our lives but the adventure of life itself that is in the process of becoming. In fact, we will not obtain the Truth, which cannot be possessed, but what matters to us above all else is to *be* true: when we are true, at least we have a chance, not of possessing the Truth, but of being *in* the Truth. Thus disarmed and without pretention, let us meet the grave challenge presented to us. Beginning from our "shared presence," to adopt Rene Char's expression, let us attempt a shared search.

For the moment, I am the only one speaking, but already an exchange is taking place as looks and thoughts intersect; soon it will be fully alive through the magic of the word that, at its best, offers the means to propel us toward the realm of infinity. That is, I know, the whole virtue of true dialogues: Socratic dialogue, Confucian dialogue, the dialogue between Abelard and Heloise, between Montaigne and La Boétie, between human and nature, between human and transcendence, between the living and the dead . . . In dialogue founded on sympathy, strewn with the unexpected and unhoped-for, the one who is speaking does not know what the interlocutor is going to say, nor what he himself will say when the interlocutor has expressed himself. Thus they advance step-by-step toward the unknown of the mind, toward the resonance of souls, toward an open in/finite. That is one more miracle: between beings marked by finitude, a joy belonging to the infinite bursts forth. And we have a vague feeling that the life truth I mentioned a moment ago must be hidden in the endless back-and-forth.

Endless? Immediately the voice of Ricaneur whispers in our ears, "But see here, *everything* has an end!" We ourselves need no convincing that in a short time we will no longer be together to extend this experience of the infinite. Thus we are left to join in the chorus of lamentations: "Vanity of vanities, all is vanity" (Ecclesiastes), "Let us pass, let us pass, since everything passes" (Apollinaire) . . . Unless we are seized by a burst of dignity that proclaims loud and strong our presences here and now. Because the fact remains, as undeniable as it is irrevocable: no longer can anything happen so that we are not here. Of course it all slips away from us. Of course we can hold on to nothing. Nevertheless one thing alone is in our possession, one thing that is not nothing: the moment. The moment of true life as in this instant. Of that we are as certain as we are of our eventual death. Alongside the certainty of death, there is in us this certainty of being the masters of the moment.

The moment is not synonymous with the present. The present is only an ordinary link in chronological time; the moment constitutes an instant that stands out in the course of our existence, a wave high above the sweep of time. Like a flash of lightning within our consciousness, the moment crystallizes our experiences of the past and our dreams of the future into an island rising out of the anonymous sea, an island lit suddenly by an intense beam of light. The moment is an instance of being in which our incessant searching suddenly encounters an echo, in which everything seems to give itself at once, once and for all. That is the special experience that the paradoxical expression "moment of eternity" conveys. This is what Friedrich Nietzsche said, cited by the poet Jean Mambrino in *L'Hespérie, pays du soir:* "Let us admit that were we saying 'yes' to a single and unique moment, we would have been saying 'yes' not only to ourselves but to all that exists. Because nothing is isolated, neither in us nor in things, and if our soul has echoed with joy even once, all the ages were necessary for creating the conditions of that single moment, and all eternity has been confirmed, justified in that unique moment when we said 'yes.'" Vaguely but deeply, we feel that the moment we have just mentioned is similar, in its breath of plenitude, to what eternity must be like.

Alluding furtively to eternity during the preceding meditation, I acknowledged that in fact no one is able to imagine how it appears. Nonetheless, however timidly, I think I may be able to say what it is not. Regarding an eternity *of life,* it is anything but an endless, monotonous repetition of the same. It must be an incredible succession of distinct instants animated by continual surges toward life. In a word, it is also made up of unique moments. In which case, the unique moments as we are able to experience them in this life, a river of diamonds or string of stars linked by memory, constitute a span that already gives us a taste of eternity. Resonating in us, Rimbaud's spontaneous song becomes our own:

> *It is found again.*
> *What? Eternity,*
> *It is the sea gone*
> *With the sun.*

Intuitively Rimbaud grasped that eternity is found in the moment, experienced in the moment, the moment of encounter when the surge toward life and life's promise coincide.

"But what is the surge toward life? And most importantly, *beginning from what* could it arise in us?" wonder so many discouraged, lost individuals who no longer know where to find the power of this surge. There is no satisfactory answer to this question, but I might risk a response nevertheless: beginning from nothing.

We must pause here to explain about this paradox, this "nothing" that we have already mentioned, which, above all, must not be confused with nothingness. Containing the promise of Everything, Nothing designates Non-Being, which is nothing other than that by which Being comes about. The notion of Non-Being is necessary because only beginning from Non-Being can we really conceive of Being.

To depict the original state of the Tao, Lao Tzu employs the terms *Hsü,* "Void," and *Wu,* "Nothing." *Wu* can be most accurately translated as "there is not" or "it is not." Chuang Tzu (fourth century BCE), the great Taoist thinker, embraces this vision when he says, "that which engenders all things cannot be a thing, Wu is beyond beings, invisible and without form." Hsü and Wu both have a dynamic aspect insofar as they are linked to the notion of Ch'i, "Breath." To be convinced of this, we need only to read the famous passage from chapter 42 of the *Tao Te Ching:*

> *The original Tao engenders the One*
> *The One engenders the Two*
> *The Two engenders the Three*

The Three engenders the Ten Thousand
> *beings*
The Ten Thousand beings leaned back
> *against Yin*
And embraced Yang
They obtained harmony through the median
> *Void.*

This passage is interpreted in the following way: from the original Tao, conceived as the supreme Void, emanates the One that is the primordial Breath, which in turn engenders the two complementary breaths Yin and Yang; through their ceaseless interaction, these two engender all the beings that succeed in creating harmony among themselves thanks to the third Breath that is the median Void. Through this interpretation we see that what is affirmed is the virtue of Nothing, of the Void, since the Void is the root of the Way, as well as being the condition of harmony in the course of the Way. To be supported by the Void is to be in keeping with the Way, which ceaselessly carries out this movement going from the Void toward the Full and returning to the Void where the primordial Breath is replenished. The proper circulation of the Way that connects all living beings comes at this price. Those who adopt this vision—followers of Taoism or Chan (Zen)—thus deeply embrace this movement and experience a fundamental truth: to be is not simply to follow the flow of an existence; it is to continually make being an active process, beginning from non-being. Ideally they experience a kind of death of self—the narrow, closed self—and attain a freer, more open form of life. Assuming that they practice calligraphy or t'ai chi, they do not doubt that the breath that enlivens them, released from the blank page by the brush stroke or from thin air by the gesture, is identical to the breath that has moved the stars since the Origin.

It would be false to believe that this great intuition is limited to Chinese or Eastern civilization, and that no inkling of it exists elsewhere. We find another quest for the Void, for example, in the Judeo-Christian tradition. Of course the context is different, since God is referred to directly. Nevertheless the two traditions have in common the idea of the death of the self, of emptying oneself in order to be filled—here with the presence of God, there with the primordial Breath. Indeed a current of thought exists in the West that has considered Nothing, the Void, particularly evident in the line inaugurated by Meister Eckhart and followed by Heinrich Suso, Johannes Tauler, Angelus Silesius, Jacob Boehme, and elsewhere by John of the Cross . . . For Meister Eckhart and his followers, Nothing, the Void, is the very posture of God, in the sense that God remains in the position of non-being even in ceaselessly performing the act of being. To be, truly to be, is never to be situated as a simple "being," already established. Rather, it is always a surging toward a state of being. That is how the Creator behaves, and his creatures likewise. Far from being negative, this vision is a most dynamic one, and it conforms to God's revelation to Moses: "I will be what I will be." Thus the truth of the Void, of Nothing, is not just a matter of abstract speculation; in truth, all the sages from all the traditions, through their very lives, attest to its effectual value.

We are now in a position to define more concretely the vital needs or irrepressible desires that the awareness of death engenders in us. Without aiming to be exhaustive, we will consider three principal ones: the desire for realization, the desire for going beyond, and the desire for transcendence.

First, the desire for realization.

The idea that life has a time limit, that it cannot be postponed, is our incentive to realize ourselves: no longer to follow a *life trajectory* that we submit to as our inescapable condition, but to conceive of a *life plan*. In other words, to project ourselves into life through a creative occupation that would lead us to the prospect of a realization. Nevertheless we recognize the sad reality: a large portion of humanity is denied the possibility of choosing an occupation and accepts work just to earn a living, a situation that leads to all kinds of suffering and injustice. Thus humans are reduced to their technical usefulness, which is a kind of mutilation for them. If we have a natural need *to make*, it is not only on the level of material production with practical use to society. It is most importantly in the dimension of what the Greeks called *poïen,* which means "to make" in the sense of *poïesis,* "creation." Through this creative "making," through work with a view to realization, we give meaning to our lives; we become the "poets" of our lives. We make sense of them. That is our vocation, our calling.

By the word *sens,* "sense," we must understand the three meanings that it has in the French language: "sensation," "direction," "significance." Compressed into one dense monosyllable like a precious stone, those three meanings somehow crystallize the three essential levels of our existence within the living universe. Between Heaven and Earth, we humans, prompted by the urgency to live, feel with all our *senses* the world that is offered to us. Attracted by what appears the most exciting, the most dazzling—the world's beauty that will be the subject of our next meditation—we advance in one direction: that is the beginning of our awareness of the Way. In the Way, all living things that push irresistibly in one *direction,* in the image of the tree that rises from its roots toward the full blossoming of its presence in the world, seem to convey an intentionality, an orientation, a need to participate that links microcosm to macrocosm. From which derives our intense attraction for *significance,* which is *le sens,* the meaning, of our realization. In other words, humans realize and realize themselves to give themselves meaning; giving themselves meaning, they give sense to their lives, because it is true that they can enjoy life most fully only through enjoyment that offers a *sense* of joy.

⟶⟵

Our awareness of death also invites us to respond to another fundamental need: the need to go beyond ourselves, which is linked to the desire for realization, but in a most exhilarating or most radical fashion.

According to whether one believes or does not believe in Heaven, death appears to some as an impassible boundary that determines the human condition and to others as a possibility for transformation. In both cases, it impales the human mind, never letting it rest, and it instills in us the need to go beyond. Death invites us to try at least to escape our ordinary condition, and that effort has a name: passion. The passion of adventure, the passion of heroism, the passion of love, as well as all kinds of other passions on a lesser scale. The ones I just named are the highest insofar as all three bring into play the life of the one who commits to them: the trial of death is the risk to be run, proof of human greatness.

With regard to adventure, I am not thinking of those who throw themselves into questionable dealings. I have in mind first of all the explorers, those great sailors, those great pilots, those intrepid climbers who reach unknown lands by confronting extreme conditions and risking their lives. I am remembering a figure near to us, endlessly admirable and captivating, the great mountaineer Chantal Mauduit. On her list of achievements, she had six triumphs over mountains with altitudes of more than eight thousand meters, among them the most difficult of the Himalayas. In 1996, upon returning to Paris after her sixth victory, she recounted her expedition on television and said among other things that on the summit, alone between Earth and Heaven, she had recited—even as she was filming herself—three lines from a poem by André Velter that she had made her profession of faith. It happened that at this exact moment, by chance, the poet was in front of his television screen. We can imagine the feeling that came over him seeing this extraordinary being whom he did not know reciting his own lines:

> *Space is an outlaw*
> *that is whom you think of*
> *when you are the gallop of your heart.*

The next day, responding to a message left by Mauduit at Radio France headquarters, Velter went to meet her. Immediately, a radiant passion united these two great lovers of life. Almost two years later, in 1998, Mauduit again heard the summits calling. For the climber, there was no gap between her carnal relationship with the body of her lover and the one she maintained with the rocks—they were of a piece. There she was halfway up the seventh mountain she had vowed to conquer. The night before the final ascent, there was an avalanche. She was buried (with her Sherpa) in the original purity, as she must have so often imagined, without wishing for it but without fearing it. The dazzling figure of Chantal Mauduit speaks to us of the great passion for adventure.

As for heroism, history provides us numerous examples. In Europe, we obviously remember the sacrifices of all those who gave their lives to free the continent from the horrifying grip of Nazism. Countless figures spring to mind here, from the young men who fell by the thousands on the beaches of Normandy or the massif of Vercors, to Father Maximilien Kolbe, the Polish Franciscan monk who willingly took the place of an actual father to suffer the collective death sentence in the concentration camp at Auschwitz. In armed combat or through extreme acts of solidarity, these heroes confronted death in the name of life, in the name of human dignity, which the Nazis wanted to annihilate. But there is another scenario that I would like to mention here, a dramatic scene that haunts the Chinese imagination.

It took place in the 1930s: During the Long March, pursued by the Nationalist Army, the Communist troops, or at least what was left of them after many defeats, arrived at the Luding Bridge, a long, narrow chain bridge suspended high above the turbulent Dadu River. Hemmed in by the mountains, this place is a veritable trap, exactly why the Nationalist command was planning to surround the Communists there to inflict upon them a definitive defeat. Less than a century before, under the reign of the Manchus, a rebel army had been annihilated at this same spot. The soldiers of the Red Army had to cross the bridge as quickly as possible or else suffer the same fate. Across the bridge the gun and cannon fire of the enemy awaited them. Zhu De, the leader, addressed his troops: "Are there volunteers to cross the bridge first?" Immediately, a hundred brave men stepped forward. Wearing grenade belts, off they charged in single file over the chains in the direction of the other bank. And in the middle of the bridge, in the rattle of gunfire and the roar of the river, one after the other, or in whole clusters, they fell, scoring the air with their vertical dives, before being swallowed by the current running red with their blood. Finally, who knows how, a few of them managed to reach the other side and to throw their grenades. Their action served to lessen the intensity of the enemy fire, thus allowing their comrades in turn to launch an attack. We can imagine today that without the action of these volunteers, the history of contemporary China would be written differently. The regime subsequently put in place by that same Red Army engendered many particularly bloody periods, but the fact remains that the sacrifice of the soldiers on the Luding Bridge, made to save the majority of their comrades from disaster, retains all its greatness. And for an example of another kind of greatness in the form of nonviolent resistance, let us remember the heroic figure of that young man in Tiananmen Square during the events of 1989, who faced a column of tanks all alone.

Life is clearly in play in the passions of adventure and heroism, but, you will ask me, what about the passion of love that, at first glance, does not seem to involve any confrontation with death? I will simply say that various cultures did not wait for psychoanalysis to name the two basic human passions, *Eros* and *Thanatos,* or to recognize the secret ties that bind them. On the Western side, as early as antiquity, the Greeks developed this theme extensively through their myths and drama. Among the Romans, Ovid subtly grasped the potential consequences of the passion of love when he said, "So I love you, so I hate you, but in vain, because I cannot not love you, so I would like to be dead with you."*

Ovid was a contemporary of the Passion of Christ. Christianity subsequently brought decisive revelations to bear on our understanding of the mystery of love. My aim here is not to plunge us into all the complexity of this problem, but simply to observe the process by which the awareness of death, through the experience of Love, in the full sense of the word, lets us discover the three constituent dimensions of our being. In fact, we have known this process forever; let us describe it briefly.

Eros has the magical power of bringing together two beings in love with one another. From a shared love, these two seek the satisfaction of their carnal desire. If they confine themselves to the single dimension of the flesh, eventually they find themselves at an impasse. By linking together those acts that each time involve excitation followed by depletion (take for example the carnal act, with its so-called small death), they link themselves together into a closed game in which the other is increasingly reified. Satisfaction becomes an exhausting enslavement that ends at best in lassitude, at worst in malevolent exacerbation that can lead to murders of passion. If, on the other hand, the two beings linked by Eros

---

*See Xavier Darcos, *Ovide et la mort* [Ovid and Death] (Paris, France: PUF, 2009).

broaden their horizons by calling upon the best of themselves, they will discover, at the end of inner efforts to get beyond themselves, other dimensions of their being, originating in the most intimate, most original and irreplaceable part of each of them, that we mean by the term *soul* at the source of all desires.

When body-to-body is enriched with soul-to-soul, love experiences a qualitative change. It inspires in each being respect and gratitude for the other. "In true love," wrote Stendhal, "it is the souls that envelop the bodies."* And addressing his beloved in a sonnet he composed, Michelangelo wrote, "I must love in you what you yourself cherish, that is, your soul." What Christianity as well as Platonism called "Agape"—one manifestation of which takes the form of courtly love—tends to replace concupiscence, sexual desire for the other, with a deeper, more open communion. In its most elevated state, the soul thus escapes the constraints of the body and of space-time by resonating with the soul of the living universe.

The Eros-Agape pairing does indeed possess a cosmic or supernatural dimension. In China, the carnal act is designated by the term *cloud-rain*.

This term originates in the legend of the sexual relationship of King Xiang of Chu with the goddess of Wu Mountain. Since then, the carnal act is experienced as intimately resonating with nature. In erotic painting, for example, instead of representing a frenetic battle scene of the flesh in a closed bedroom, the preference is for depicting the act unfolding in

---

*Cited by Jean Mambrino, *L'Hespérie, pays du soir* [Hesperia, the Evening Land] (Paris, France: Arfuyen, 2000).

a room with a window opening to the outside where blossoming branches and chirping birds appear, caressed by the spring breeze or haloed in moonlight. In cases where the room is shown closed, there is at least a folding screen representing a landscape. That makes me think of Proust's subtle words: "Love is space and time rendered perceptible to the heart."

In all cultures Eros-Agape links the human to the divine. The ecstasy that it provides is often identified with mystical ecstasy—one of the most beautiful illustrations of this is surely the Song of Songs. All the same, in the face of the divine, taking stock of our mortal condition, we humans aspire to transcendence through a lasting love that death cannot interrupt. That spoilsport death thus becomes the very criterion by which we may judge the authenticity of love: love must be "as strong as death," according to the expression from the Song of Songs, and it must be able to confront it and cross it to be accepted as authentic. In this as well, all cultures have emblematic figures of such crossings, like Tristan and Isolde. Lovers possessing a lasting love know their finitude even as they are sure that, beyond their individual selves, their love will never end. This startling apprehension of the mystery of love is expressed by the philosopher Gabriel Marcel thus: "To love a being is to say, 'You, you will not die.'"

The third and final fundamental desire that the awareness of death invites us to realize: our striving toward transcendence. I will address it here briefly, before coming back to it in the last meditation.

I agree with Chateaubriand when he states that "it is through death that morality entered life." Like Simone Weil,

I am convinced that without the trial of suffering and death, we would have not have had the idea of God, nor even the least thought of transcendence. Let me be clear however that it is not death in itself that acts directly upon us, but the awareness we have of it. The truth is that death has no power in itself; it is only the cessation of a certain state of life. When buoyed by hope, we exclaim as Saint Paul did, "Death, where is your victory, where is your sting?" But we know that our cry can only be heard by the living; the dead will never hear it. As we have seen, death seems to reign as master of the world, but its power can only be conferred upon it originally by that absolute which is life, and which, in order to be life, requires bodily death. Life does not belong to us, rather we belong to it. It is transcendent for the simple reason that even as it pulses through the deepest part of us, it is infinitely above and beyond us. We have no choice but to recognize that there is a sacred order of Life from which the living universe proceeds, and that man, being prey to evil, can be neither the measure of the universe nor the measure of himself. Having become a being of mind, he becomes mind; that is why we can say: man surpasses man. Plato understood clearly that only the divine dimension, involving absolute Good, allows man to achieve his full measure, provided of course that man not take himself for the divine. Nothing is more dangerous than a relativist humanism that establishes the criterion of man within man. All abuses are then allowed. In relationship to the sacred order of Life, we have only to trust ourselves to it in complete confidence. And we can do this because experience shows us that the Breath that brought about Life has never failed, and will never fail. Moreover, our true bond with others—the bond of friendship or love based on unfailing confidence as well—is only possible in the light of this transcendence.

In China, since antiquity, there resounds a short phrase passed down from generation to generation, a phrase drawn originally from the *I Ching, The Book of Changes,* the first work of Chinese thought, compiled a thousand years before our era, and to which both Taoism and Confucianism refer. This expression is composed of four characters, percussive as four clashes of the cymbals: *Sheng-sheng-pu-hsi,* "Life engenders life, there will be no end." This maxim has allowed the Chinese people to survive countless bloody conflicts and catastrophes.

The human, a small being lost within the universe, deserves much credit. Despite everything, humans have carried and continue to carry the torch of life. Entering life, they must face trials coming from all the levels of the surrounding world as well as their own beings: biological, psychological, ethical, and spiritual. In these trials, the supreme trial being death, they experience pain and suffering. There is undeniable greatness in that. Beyond the trials, joys are nevertheless granted them, carnal as well as spiritual joys, crowned by a great mystery, the mystery of love. Without love, no pleasure achieves its full meaning; with love, which involves the whole being, everything is taken care of: the body, the mind, and the soul.

With regard to this body-soul-mind triptych, I would like to provide further explanation, because confusion often reigns over the respective status of the last two terms. They are often used interchangeably in our times, and usually to the detriment of the specific nature of the soul, to the point that its very existence is frequently called into question. Despite the enduring presence of the term in the French language (*en mon âme et conscience,* in all honesty; *avoir l'âme chevillée au corps,* to hang onto life; *supplément d'âme,* a little something extra; *l'âme soeur,* soul sister, and so on), many are content with the body-mind pair to designate the fundamental components of the human being.

Nonetheless, in the West as in many other cultures, an age-old tradition has detected in each human being something outside the scope of the mind alone, something intimate, something secret that is his or her own; which includes that being's astonishing capacity to feel, to be moved, but also an unconscious part never completely elucidated; which, buried in the inner depths of one's being, indivisible, constitutes the very mark of her or his uniqueness. This idea, so long present in the Western tradition but now lost, expresses an instinctive effort to go beyond the dualism established by the body-mind pair by introducing this third element whereby humans can communicate unhindered with the soul of the universe.

Chinese thought would willingly consent to this effort, having always preferred a three-way process for explaining how human life is constituted and functions. We will recall that Taoism, based on the idea of the Breath, proposes an interaction between Yin, Yang, and the median Void, whereas Confucianism is based on the interdependent relationship of Heaven, Earth, and Human. Thus, according to the Chinese tradition, every human being is constituted from three components: the *ching,* the sperm, the *ch'i,* the breath, and the *shen,* the divine. Although this is not an exact word-for-word equivalence, we can generally associate the *ching* with the body, the *ch'i* with the mind, and the *shen* with the soul.

A complementary or dialectical relationship is established

between the soul and the mind. If the soul is intimately personal, the mind has a more general, collective aspect; it is the mind that allows for language and reason. The role of the mind is central: it helps to form the individual and to locate him or her within the social network. The soul participates in the essence of each being, constituting its most secret and sometimes least conscious part; it is there, intact, from before birth, and it accompanies that being, still intact, to the final state, even if the mind is altered or fails. Patiently absorbing all the gifts and the trials of the body and the mind, the soul is the authentic fruit conserving intact what constitutes the uniqueness of each individual.

On the concrete level, the mind calls upon the brain, the soul functions from the heart. The mind is apprehended by the intellect, the soul is grasped by intuition. That is why I was once able to write that "the mind moves, the soul is moved; the mind reasons, the soul resonates."* That is why we can also note in life at large a kind of division of labor the two of them maintain: the mind governs language, philosophical thought, scientific inquiry, and all social organizations (politics, economics, law, education, health, and so on); as for the soul, it has the last word on everything that concerns emotion, artistic creation, and the mystical dimension of human destiny in its open relationship with the beyond or the transcendent, which is manifest through resonance. All human aspiration toward absolute love is concentrated there, all possibility of our connection to the divine.

Becoming a being of mind and granted a soul, the human is in a position to participate in the higher orders of life.

---

*See the article "Âme" in the journal *Europe*, no. 1000 (2012).

Taoist thought recognizes life's many orders when it asserts that "man proceeds from Earth, Earth proceeds from Heaven, Heaven proceeds from the Tao, and the Tao proceeds from itself." On the Western side we can understand in a new, non-dogmatic, and truly universal way Pascal's words on the three orders. Let us agree to listen to him, even if some of us may feel uncomfortable with the word *charity* that he uses to designate divine love. Far from the pejorative and clerical connotations that this word can convey, for him, this love is a passion permeated with limitless compassion. Such a passion cannot result from simple instinct or reason; it is of another order. At least let us recognize the need to distinguish the orders, because only this distinction allows us to grasp the potential future of the great adventure mentioned earlier.

Let us listen: "All bodies, the firmament, the stars, the earth and its realms are not worth the least of minds; because the mind knows all that, and itself, and bodies know nothing. All the bodies together, and all the minds together, and all they produce are not worth the least movement of charity. Charity is of an infinitely higher order. From all the bodies together, one could not manage to produce the least thought; that is impossible and of another order. From all the bodies and minds, one could not derive any movement of true charity; that is impossible, and of another, supernatural, order."

THIRD MEDITATION

Dear friends, the course that I have followed justifies the title of these meditations on death, *in other words on life*. Because to think about death is to think about life. The awareness of death, which prompts in us the idea that life is sacred, gives life all its value. Beginning from this awareness that never leaves him, man enters into his destiny which opens onto a series of qualitative, ascending actions and transformations. From this new perspective, and with the coming of each infant into the world, human life reveals itself to be an adventure full of promise and the unknown.

I am speaking of the awareness of death and not death itself. As you will have understood by now, I am not in the least praising death. On the contrary, it is a matter of gaining more clarity on life, of living more fully.

Along the paths of existence we come up against two fundamental mysteries, the mystery of beauty and the mystery of evil. Beauty is mysterious because the universe was not obliged to be beautiful. Whereas it happens that it is, and that seems to reveal a desire, an appeal, a hidden intentionality that can leave no one indifferent. Evil is mysterious as well. If evil presented itself to us only in the form of a few flaws or failures, due to life's difficult progress, we could accept it more or less. But among humans it achieves such radical heights that it approaches the absolute. When human cleverness is put to the service of evil, human cruelty knows no bounds. And we now know that, with the help of technology, the work of evil undertaken by humans can destroy the order of life itself. These two mysteries, which intrude upon our awareness of death, rise up before us as inescapable challenges that we have to accept. We will take a hard look at them, one after the other, beauty first.

The universe was not obliged to be beautiful, as I have said. We can imagine a universe being simply functional, a neutral system that would develop without the least touch of beauty. Such a universe would be content to run in neutral, to set in motion a collection of neutral, undifferentiated elements, moving indefinitely. We would be dealing with a world of robots, a kind of enormous machine or a concentration camp world, but in any case, we would no longer be in the order of life. In order for life to exist, elements at the cellular level must be differentiated, grow complex, and consequently form each being's singularity. The law of life requires that each being constitute an organic whole and at the same time possess the capacities of growth and transmission. That is why the immense adventure of life results in each blade of grass, each insect, each one of us. Through its uniqueness, each being tends toward the fullness of its presence in the world, in the way of a flower or a tree. That is where the very definition of beauty begins.

It would be in bad faith not to admit that the living universe is beautiful. Even if we do not know how to interpret it, that is a fact: the world is beautiful and its beauty inhabits the least of its nooks and crannies—a stream singing among the irises, an orange tree in the middle of a courtyard—just as it appears in large entities like glaciers, deserts, mountains, the sea, the meadow undulating in the breeze, the sky shimmering with stars . . . And then there is all that falls within the interval, the interstice, the intersection, the encounter: a dragonfly that lingers on a trembling reed, a lizard crossing a lichen-covered rock, sunset's rays highlighting a section of old wall, and among humans, sometimes, an exchange of looks more searing than lightning . . . As fascinating as it is intriguing, such beauty seems be a signal to us that the universe is desirable and meaningful. Thanks to beauty, nature imposes itself upon us not as an anonymous face but as a presence. As a result, each of us, striving toward beauty, finds our uniqueness also transformed into presence.

What strikes us immediately is the beauty of the cosmos and of nature, and within nature, the beauty of living beings. But within the human realm specifically, we perceive other types of beauty. Immediately, the physical beauty of humans possesses something extra: it is animated by the awareness of beauty, or more, by the surge toward beauty. That is to say, up to a certain level it is already shaped by the mind. At a higher level, beyond that physical beauty, resides the beauty of the heart and the soul. Spiritual beauty, wholly internal, is no longer defined by external traits but is revealed through looks and gestures. A passionate look, transparent, loving, and captivating, a gesture of affection, generosity, tenderness, comfort, sacrifice—a gift in other words—all that falls under the higher order of the beauty of the heart and soul whose source is the original Gift and whose expression is friendship and love. When selfless friendship and love are raised to the universal, they constitute the highest realization of humanity. Because the original Gift evokes the advent of Life itself, it goes back to the original, divinely inspired *beau geste*.

It is for all this beauty that we become attached to the world and to life. It is what persuades us, often without our knowing it, that life is worth the trouble of living it. But there is a catch: with regard to beauty, a certain prejudice hardens us against it. We cannot trust it without reservations. We are afraid of being victims of illusions. How often beauty seems to deceive us! And we see that in the hands of those with bad intentions, it can become an instrument of domination, even destruction. That is because, endowed with intelligence and freedom, humans are capable of corrupting everything, and that includes using beauty's power of seduction as a tool. Thus, for whoever sets out to study beauty, the first task must be to distinguish its essence from the uses to which it can be put.

Those abuses must not keep us from admiring beauty, which is essentially good, but they can serve as a constant reminder to us that there can be no aesthetics without ethics. That is why in many languages (Sanskrit, Chinese, and so on) beauty and goodness share the same root. In my book *The Way of Beauty,* we lingered long over the bonds between these two qualities that reside in the human soul. Let us recall what Henri Bergson said, "The highest degree of beauty is grace, but in the word 'grace' we hear goodness as well. Because supreme goodness is that generosity of a life principle that offers itself indefinitely. That is the very meaning of grace." To this masterful philosophical formulation, I proposed the following response: "Goodness is the guarantee of the quality of beauty; as for beauty, it illuminates goodness and makes it desirable."

Why does beauty have anything to do with death? First of all because, like everything else, it cannot last, it escapes us. And since we become more attached to it than to anything in life, the deeper the attachment, the more wrenching the loss. Attachment-loss: that is the condition of beauty; it sharpens our awareness of death. And all the more so because its mode of existence is not static; it manifests itself each time in its appearance on the crest of the moment. And above all there is the fact that, when it is sublime, it inspires a sacred fear or a passion too fervent for our human capacity to fulfill completely. Like the sun, we cannot look directly into it without risking our eyesight or our life. Those who know the high plateaus of the Himalayas, at four thousand meters, understand their inhabitants' urgent need to prostrate themselves before the mountains ablaze with eternal whiteness and rising to an altitude of more than eight thousand meters. Those who know the vast night in the desert understand the nomads who kneel down and pray, dazzled by the blinding flames of the stars. When Dante saw Beatrice for the first time, at nine years old, he felt the spirit of life begin to throb so strongly within him that it almost ruptured his veins. When, nine years later, at three o'clock in the afternoon one day he saw her again and heard her voice greet him for the first time, he believed he had touched the furthest limit of bliss. And he knew that whatever remained could only be fulfilled beyond this life.

In view of what we have just said, the one who sets out to confront beauty in order to make a work of art, that is, the artist, confronts the challenge of death at the same time. And that is all the more true since artistic creation is precisely one of the forms by which man tries to triumph over his mortal destiny. Any artwork worthy of that name—poetry, music, painting, sculpture—attempts to transmute solitude into opening, suffering into communion, cries for help into song, a song that resonates beyond the chasms widened by separation and death.

Authentic artistic creation, in the West as elsewhere, follows the Orphic route, the one that bears the marks of dead Eurydice, the one by which Orpheus tries to rejoin her now by means of another type of incantation. To consider only one Western example, let us recall Victor Hugo addressing his daughter Léopoldine, four years after her death:

> Tomorrow, at dawn, at the hour when the
> countryside whitens,
> I will set out. You see, I know you are
> waiting for me.
> I will go through the forest, I will go through
> the mountains,
> I can no longer remain far from you . . .

These are words of Orphic inspiration, of returning to the dead, that have become so close to us all. Later, delivering a speech at the grave of his son's fiancé, the same poet

will say, "The wonder of this great celestial departure called
death is that those who leave have not gone away at all. They
are in a world of light, but they are present, tender witnesses
to our world of darkness. They are high up and very close.
Oh! Whoever you may be, you who have watched a dear one
vanish into the tomb, do not believe that he has left you. He
is still there. He is beside you more than ever. The beauty of
death is presence, the inexpressible presence of beloved souls,
smiling at the tears in our eyes. The one we mourn is dead,
not gone. We no longer perceive his sweet face; we feel ourselves under his wing. The dead are invisible, but they are not
absent . . ."

In China, the equivalent of the tradition inaugurated
by Orpheus was embodied first by Ch'ü Yüan in the fourth
century BCE and later by all the artists embracing the spirit
of Chan according to which being passes through non-being,
seeing through non-seeing, speaking through non-speaking.
To illustrate the voice/way of Chan, here are two quatrains by
Wang Wei, an eighth-century poet:

> *At the ends of branches, magnolia blossoms*
> *In the heart of the mountains offer their red*
>   *calyxes.*
> *(The dwelling near the waterfalls is silent, no*
>   *one there.)*
> *The first open out while the second descend.*

In this poem, the third line is in parentheses to indicate
to us that there is not a living soul in this landscape, while
in reality the poet is very much there since he is witnessing
the whole scene. But through the practice of asceticism, he is

in a state of non-being, and it is only in this state that he is in a position to integrate the great law of transformation, by which all death moves toward rebirth.

> *Empty mountain. No one in sight;*
> *Only a few voices can still be heard.*
> *Returning rays penetrate the deep woods;*
> *Once again they light the green moss.*

Over the course of his mountain walks, says this second quatrain, the poet enters into a state of emptiness, like the mountain that empties itself toward evening. In the third line, the "returning rays" refer to the rays of the setting sun that glance back to light the Earth and signify the human glancing back, in the spiritual sense. The poet only has to look back (like Orpheus?) to see something other than the simple end of the day, to see that the light does not disappear; it illuminates what is hidden in the depths—the "green moss" representing the presence of the original place.

Thus the artist, more than others, must be situated in the Double Realm. There he captures the moment when dawn shatters the darkness of night, without forgetting the moment when the last ray of the setting sun fades behind the mountains. He praises nature in full flower without ignoring winter forever present in the branches that remember the time when they were numb, stripped of their leaves. He celebrates the fact of living here and now, even in *re-creating* that which seemed lost. In doing so, the creator puts himself in the position of the Creator who, let us recall, made Everything beginning from Nothing. Thus, the artistic way, in its highest dimension, reconnects the human to the divine.

Nevertheless let us not forget all the artists and poets who did not want to follow the models of harmony and sought beauty in something other than formal equilibrium. There is often greatness in their quest that passes through dissonance, asymmetry, and even the grotesque. Even beyond the questions of form, some have rightly studied the role of chaos and decay itself that can be at the heart of our existence. Those artists who have tried to look hard at decomposition and death deserve credit as pioneers even if their modernity later devolved into complaisant nihilism. Let us take the poem "Carrion" by Baudelaire. It depicts the putrid carcass of an animal decaying under the sun, given over like a "lewd woman" to the appetite of black battalions of grubs. Then the poet reflects with horror that the woman whom he adores will one day be reduced to that state. His only consolation is that, even so, he will have saved "the form and divine essence" of her present beauty. This poem can inspire in us two feelings, apparently contradictory but actually complementary. On the one hand, we can lament the fragility or even the vanity of beauty and find confirmation that physical beauty is not enough. On the other hand, we can also be seized by the incredible fact that beauty nevertheless exists, that despite so precarious a condition, doomed to degradation, this miracle continues to be incarnated. Thus we may think of Chuang Tzu who affirms in the last chapter of his book, *The Book of Chuang Tzu,* that "between heaven and earth there is great beauty" and celebrates "the magic power of nature that never ceases to transmute decay into marvel."

At the heart of the artist's creation—which is a headlong struggle or fight with the angel—lies the same type of experience as passionate love, but more bitter no doubt since it requires mastering a form. Whether it is harmonious as with Vermeer or convulsive as with Francis Bacon, art requires that an exact intensity be achieved, animated by the rhythmic breath. For that to happen the artist is led to call fully upon the three components of his being: body, mind, and soul.

I explained my understanding of these three components in the previous meditation. Allow me to continue with this theme in order to apply it specifically to the area of artistic creation. The body forms the base of everything and artistic creation begins with bodily contact with the world. More than contact, it is a matter of true interaction between the internal world of the artist and all that the external world can offer him or her in the way of materials and inspiration. In this interaction, the mind is already at work, because there is an eminently conscious "making" involved in technical mastery, as well as a relevant understanding of potential themes. But in the end it is a deep, intimate, entirely personal vision that the artist must try hard to achieve. That is where the soul comes in. As we have seen, the soul is the most secret part of each being; since our birth or even before, it keeps alive a light that wants to shine, a cradlesong that would love to make itself heard. Jacques de Bourbon-Busset was right to define it as the "continuo of each being." In its highest state, every work of art resonates from soul to soul with other beings and with Being. That is the way for each creator to overcome space-time, to transcend separation and death. The aim is not communication but communion.

As we advance in age, the soul further internalizes all that the body bears of desires and experiences. As I have said, the fruit of the soul absorbs pain and joy, blood and tears. Artists are no exception here. The closer they come to the end, the more their creations are stripped down and freed. Let us consider Michelangelo's final pietà, the last portraits by Titian and Rembrandt, the final visions of someone like Fan Kuan or Cézanne. Think of Dante's *Divine Comedy,* Racine's *Phaedra,* the last poems of Tu Fu, Wang Wei, Rumi, Tagore. Consider the final cantatas of Bach, Beethoven's last quartets, and Shubert's last sonatas, the requiems by Mozart and Fauré . . . Nor have I forgotten Mahler's *Song of the Earth* or the last four lieder by Richard Strauss, nostalgic cries as glorious as the glory of the setting sun itself. Moreover, we each know what music we would like to hear at the moment of death.

Let us listen: combining empty and full, alternately surging and subsiding, an uninterrupted song rises from the earth and rejoins the great rhythm of the eternal current that moves the stars. Rhythm differs from cadence, which is a repetition of the same; rhythm is the interaction of vital breaths in all its complexity: advance and reprise, reprise and advance again, syncopated clashing, harmonious intertwining, spiraling movement changing register and dimension, bringing about transformation and transfiguration whereby the effect of death, to quote Claudel's phrase in *The Satin Slipper,* is the "deliverance of captive souls."

⌒⌒⌒

Unfortunately, something in being prevents that music. Humans have given that essential flaw a name: evil.

With regard to beauty, we have seen that humans, endowed with intelligence and freedom, are capable of corrupting everything. That is all the more evident with regard to death, which clearly lends itself to corruption. Prompted by poorly controlled instincts, destructive instincts, sexual

instincts, moved by hate or jealousy, the madness of possession or domination, man does not hesitate to make death
his radical instrument in the service of evil. When someone
who possesses the power of life and death over others exercises that power, not only can he take the lives of his victims,
before doing away with them, he can use threats or torture
to humiliate and debase them to the point of robbing them
of everything human. Thus he kills their very souls. He creates a true nothingness that the living universe, as it runs its
course, certainly had not anticipated. He creates something
like a black hole in the realm of the living.

In the order of life, humans, as beings of the highest
capabilities—capable of selfless and universal love—could
almost have broken the terrible chain that consists of killing
to survive. But in the reality of our history we reveal ourselves to be the most disturbing, if not terrifying, animal.
Conversely, the animals we have domesticated according to
a few sound principles, such as the horse, dog, camel, mule,
donkey, and rabbit, retain virtues that many men have for-
saken: nobility, fidelity, patience, gentleness, innocence. All
that human ingenuity we so admire (and therein lies one of
the arguments often used to demonstrate humankind's supe-
riority), producing all the technology that has seen exponen-
tial growth in modern times, has also experienced the worst
deviations as it has advanced. It has allowed further refinement of torture methods, more efficient mass exterminations,
and the creation of concentration camps. In the twentieth
century, we saw on display a whole spectrum of methods of
killing invented by man, from the most primitive to the most
sophisticated, on the individual level as well as the collective
level. Who among us can imagine or feel all the suffering of

that young man in the hands of the "Gang of Barbarians," as they called themselves, or that young woman in the hands of sadists for interminable days and nights in a filthy cellar up to the moments of their deaths? And when hatred takes possession of the masses, driving them to massacre, no barrier is strong enough to hold back their fury and contempt. We have witnessed executioners during some massacres, because of economic considerations or to save time, forcing their victims to dig wide pits before pushing them in with their rifle butts or bayonets and then burying them alive. In other cases, we have witnessed victims begging to be shot instead of being slashed with machetes and their executioners shouting back, "Bullets for scum like you? Ha!" During another ethnic cleansing, this time very close to us, we witnessed children assassinated in front of their mothers before the mothers themselves were killed, we saw women raped in front of their husbands before the husbands were finished off. Terrible, terrible twentieth century that erased from its pediments the supreme law of respect for life!*

"You shall not kill" is an implicit commandment that holds in all cultures. Still it deserves to be stated out loud. That is the case in the Hebrew tradition where this commandment is a holy order issued from On High. All human society is based on a few fundamental prohibitions, the first being the ban on incest, but "You shall not kill" is the most

---

*Notes from the editor: In this paragraph the author refers to a case in France in 2006 in which a group of people, the "Gang of Barbarians," kidnapped, brutally tortured, and eventually murdered Ilan Halimi, a young French-Jewish man, on the grounds that "all Jews are rich," believing they would be able to get a large ransom from his family. Later in the paragraph the author implicitly refers to the genocide in Rwanda and the ethnic cleansing during the Bosnian war to stand for the universal horrors of all wars.

fundamental. Thus, less than thirty years after the monstrous carnage of World War II when I heard ringing out among us the offhand "It is forbidden to forbid!" it frightened me. Of course we must struggle against all oppressive and unjust prohibitions. But the margin between that and wiping the slate clean of all limits is the very one that separates civilization from barbarism. Because it is the law of life that frees us, and not the rule of anything goes. To confuse true freedom, the guarantee of human dignity, with an anything-goes attitude governed solely by the principle of pleasure is a deadly mistake. What frightened me most in that period was that nowhere did I hear the great intellectuals rising to denounce this nonsense. Carefully reading many "masters of thinking" whose superb intelligence was to be admired, I realized that their thoughts ended with the same conclusion: "Everything is permitted." How not to think of Dostoyevsky who, frightened by the nascent nihilism at the end of the nineteenth century, warned, "If God does not exist, everything is permitted."

The end of the twentieth century announced not only the death of God but also the death of man. For the one making this announcement, was it a simple observation or a new warning? In the second case, we had a right to expect renewed efforts to introduce values again into the ethical domain. That expectation was not fulfilled. The truth is that when any notion of the sacred is banished, it is impossible for humans to establish a true hierarchy of values. Thus we can try to impose a few rules externally, but in vain: the soul will not embrace them on a fundamental level because they do not come from a true source of life, nor are they fed by one.

Such a will to dissolve any notion of limit proceeded from a will toward desacralization in general. I believe it was a grave mistake, because a world without the sacred is a world of chaos. That is why we should reaffirm what is fundamentally sacred: life. And at the same time we should affirm that each individual's death is sacred as well—death understood again to be the inalienable fruit of each individual's destiny according to his mandate from Heaven. We have almost forgotten what the specialists on prehistory have taught us, that is, attending to the future of our dead individually characterizes the beginnings of the hominid. We have almost failed to admire Antigone simply for her courageous act against the reason of State, forgetting that if she consents to the sacrifice it is to proclaim that divine law dictates a decent burial for each individual. She reminds Creon, and us all, that the care of a dead body falls under a transcendence taking precedence over all human laws.

All murders violate the flesh of their victims and deprive them of their own deaths. Mass murders worsen this effect of dispossession of death that is equivalent to dehumanization. Human history shows no lack of such tragic events, but those of the twentieth century increased in horror by several degrees because of the abuses of technology as mentioned above. In the case of the genocide perpetrated by the Nazis, murder was pushed to the final limits. The Nazis carried out an industrialization of death with a coldblooded rationality, depriving death of all meaning: death no longer had anything to do with being human, since it was the work of a factory that produced thousands of corpses daily, every day for months and years, in ceaseless terror. That death which I have called one of our most precious possessions died at Auschwitz. When millions of bodies of men, women, and children are reduced to ashes, or worse, used as raw materials (women's hair, gold teeth, human fat made into soap . . .), yes, we can say that death was killed. Moreover, the Nazis' brand of murder did not merely organize the extermination of a people, it aimed at making everything conspire so that the extermination itself would be exterminated, so that forever after no one would be able to remember the annihilated lives, as though they had never existed. Their deaths, like their lives, were to be lost forever in the Night and the Fog.

The collapse of Hitler's regime did not allow time to obliterate all the piles of emaciated bodies, all the heaps of nameless skeletons. If we were to try to forget them on the pretext that their image is too unbearable to allow us to live happily, then we would become accomplices in the murders. Fortunately, there are still many of us left to see a soul behind each emaciated body, a soul like that of the poet Benjamin Fondane for example, who died at Auschwitz in 1944:

> It is to you that I speak, men on the other side
>   of the world,
> I speak man to man,
> with the little of me that remains human,
> with the little voice that remains in my
>   throat,
> my blood is on the roads, can't it cry, can't it
>   cry vengeance!
> [. . .]
> A day will come, that's certain, of quenched
>   thirst,
> we will be beyond memory, death
> will have perfected the works of hatred,
> I will be a bouquet of nettles under your feet,
> —then, ah well, know that I had a face

as you do. A mouth that prayed, as you do.
[. . .]
And yet, no!
I was not a man like you.
You were not born on the roads,
no one threw your little ones into the sewers
like kittens with their eyes still closed,
you did not wander from city to city,
hounded by the police,
you never knew the disasters at dawn,
the cattle trucks
and the bitter sob of humiliation,
accused of a crime that you did not commit,
a murder for which the corpse is still missing,
changing name and face
so as not to bear a name that people booed,
a face that served as everyone's spittoon!*

Like Fondane, all victims experienced extreme pain and grief, extreme solitude and endless despair, and nevertheless, at the moment of the ultimate test, many of them called out the name of a beloved. They had retained their entire sense of humanity, while their executioners annihilated themselves in vile inhumanity.

Such an evocation of absolute evil and the unspeakable suffering that it caused, and that it causes still, leaves us speechless. I have just one thing to say about it: it is my deep conviction that if the world should one day be saved, it will be saved with all its innocent victims.

---

*Pierre Seghers, *La Résistance et ses poètes* [The Resistance and Its Poets] (Paris, France: Seghers, 2004).

FOURTH MEDITATION

Dear friends, over the course of my previous meditations we came to see that life imposed bodily death as one of its own laws in order for life to be life, for life to become life. Since death is only the cessation of a certain state of life, it would not exist if life did not exist. Bodily death, ineluctable as it is, paradoxically reveals life to be the real absolute principle. There is only one single adventure, that of life. Nothing can change the fact that this adventure has come about in the universe and will continue. In saying so, I am not thinking only of those followers of all religions who do not doubt this truth. I refer as well to those who earnestly adhere to the facts. I am thinking of Spinoza affirming that "the essence of life is eternal." I am thinking of the Chinese with no particular belief who made their adage the one I have already cited: "Life engenders life, there will be no end." This assertion is based on the idea that the Way is an adventure in the midst of becoming, according to the law of transformation in multiple dimensions, and that all earthly experience, rather than being pure loss, can become vital material for attaining another order of life.

Life as an adventure in becoming, full of the potential for transformation and metamorphosis . . . That being the case, let us finally pose the question that is burning our tongues: What about individual death? What about the dream of eternal life that each of us secretly harbors? What hope does it allow us? Having become beings of language and mind, we know that this line of questioning will find no answers with respect to our physical bodies, clearly destined to decay. Must we turn then to the soul, that undeniably unique and irreplaceable part of each being, capable of absorbing into it the gifts of the body and the mind? Is the survival of the soul a conceivable prospect? Do not expect me to answer this question like a judge pronouncing a sentence. Moreover, no one can do that, precisely for the simple reason that life itself is an adventure in becoming. I am not here lecturing but meditating, and very humbly, in your company. I am trying to advance step by step keeping as close as possible to the truth.

First let us consider the idea that at the moment of a person's death, the soul is released from the body and survives it. This idea remains fixed in all religions and still thrives in many cultures. We know for example that in Islam, the Last Judgment is the supreme Event (*al-Waqi'a*) that justifies the Resurrection as a new Creation; each soul then knows the reality of God and its own value. As for Hinduism, let us hear the teaching of Ramana Maharshi: "The existence of each individual is evident, with or without body, as much in the state of waking as in dream or deep sleep. Thus why wish to remain chained by the body? Let man find his eternal Self, die, and be immortal and happy."

Now let us look at the case of China. In ancient times this relatively nonreligious people adhered instinctively to a belief in the lasting nature of the soul. Moreover the ideogram *hun*, "soul," contains the element that designates the spirits or shades over whom death has no power. In about the fourth century BCE, the notion of soul found a more precise formulation composed of two complementary parts: *hun*, "light or reasonable soul," and *p'o*, "dark or sensitive soul." Upon a person's death, the light soul attains Heaven and the dark soul rejoins Earth. This vision remains roughly that of Taoism. Later Buddhism introduced the idea of reincarnation. Both of these religions are concerned with ensuring that the souls of the deceased do not get lost or become wandering souls—prayers are offered to that effect. In contemporary China society is at the point of being turned upside down so that everything has become confused, especially after decade-long campaigns launched by Communist ideologues against all forms of "superstitions." But strangely, even among these resolute materialists, it is not uncommon at the funerals of important revolutionary figures for banners or signs to appear, bearing inscriptions like "His spirit remains alive forever" or "His heroic soul is not dead." And feeling his time approaching, Mao Tse-tung himself repeated on many occasions, "Soon I am going to see Marx."

In the West, where Platonism and the whole Judeo-Christian tradition have left their mark, the notion of the immortal soul was widely accepted at least until the middle of the eighteenth century, when it was countered more and more systematically by atheism. Nevertheless the debate between the atheists and those whose vision of life incorporates the dimension of a beyond is not always so clear-cut, since the agnostics come between them. Thus we should add some nuances to our observation. It occurs to me here to mention some specific events that have to do with the soul and the communion of souls, events that have touched me personally.

When you go from France into Italy along the Mediterranean coast, past Genoa and La Spezia, you follow the Liguria coast, passing through a series of small towns, ancient fishing ports built into the mountain, each coiled at the end of a perfectly curved bay. This series of bays forms what is called the "Gulf of Poets," because this astonishingly beautiful spot has been haunted since ancient times by generations of poets beginning with Virgil and Dante. In the early nineteenth century, two English poets came to join that long Italian line, and two important ones at that: George Byron and Percy Bysshe Shelley. Shelley, with his wife Mary—who would later be known for inventing the character of Frankenstein—took up residence in Lerici in the company of a couple of friends. The two couples lived in a large, luminous white patrician house, with a lush green hill above it. The house was on a path that led to the village, and just on the other side of it lay the beach. There Shelley experienced total immersion in the beauty of nature, devoting himself to intense literary endeavors—he translated Plato, Aeschylus, Spinoza, Goethe . . . There too he was in continual revolt against English society and tormented as well by his divided passion for his wife Mary and Jane, who came to visit with friends and to whom he devoted sublime verses. It was in this context that the news reached him of the death of another poet of genius, John Keats, in Rome under painful and wretched conditions. Given a terribly rough time by the critics, wasted away by tuberculosis, Keats had had to flee England as well. Deeply distressed, Shelley began to compose a great elegy, an Orphic song dedicated to Keats, fifty-five stanzas long and entitled "Adonais." It remains his best known work. Let us read the last stanza:

> The breath whose might I have invoked in
> song
> Descends on me; my spirit's bark is driven,
> Far from the shore, far from the trembling
> throng
> Whose sails were never to the tempest given;
> The massy earth and sphered skies are riven!
> I am borne darkly, fearfully, afar;
> Whilst, burning through the inmost veil of
> Heaven,
> The soul of Adonais, like a star,
> Beacons from the abode where the Eternal
> are.

We should note that Shelley was an avowed atheist, whereas for Keats "the earth is a valley where souls grow." Even so, their specific convictions do not really matter. In this last stanza, Shelley is moved by the desire to rejoin the soul of Keats watching over the abode of the Eternal ones: "The soul of Adonais, like a star, / Beacons from the abode where the Eternal are."

Rejoin the soul of Keats, but how? By way of water. Because on Keats's tombstone in Rome is engraved: "Here lies one whose name was writ in water." As though by intuition, Shelley says in his poem, "my spirit's bark is driven/ Far from the shore" and later: "I am borne darkly, fearfully, afar" toward the beacon that is Adonais's soul. Intuition or premonition? Less than a year later, accompanied by a friend, Shelley went out to sea for a sail. A storm struck, the sailboat was shipwrecked, and the poet's body tossed up on a beach near Viareggio. In his jacket was found a collection of Keats's poems. The poet's friends and loved ones, among them Byron, hastily gathered. A pyre was built on that very beach and the body cremated. That evening while the flames rose toward the starlit sky, Byron, shattered by grief, dove into the sea and swam until his strength gave out.

I became aware of Western literature at the age of fifteen, beginning precisely with English poetry. Portraits of Keats and Shelley adorned the walls of my room. Keats died at twenty-six, Shelley at thirty. As I have said, I did not think I would live as long as they did. In that period I came upon a poem one day that Shelley had written high in the Apennines. Seated on a rock, surrounded by the scent of pines and the humming of bees, the poet contemplated the Mediterranean Sea in the distance glistening in the summer afternoon sun. I was seized by a fierce desire to one day experience that same scene. Now I was in the depths of China in the midst of a time of war. I had never seen the sea and never imagined visiting it one day, to say nothing of the far-off Mediterranean! I do not know by what miracle I was eventually able to come to Europe. I became a French poet and my poems were translated into Italian, notably by another poet, Michele Baraldi, who is here today. That is how I found myself winning the prestigious Lerici Pea Award for Poetry. That was in 2009, the year I turned eighty. Lerici! You can imagine my feelings at finding myself, as though in a dream, in that place formerly inhabited by the tutelary figures of my adolescence.

From the balcony of my room I had a view of the white house which was always there, intact, in the freshness of dawn, in the incandescence of noon, in the glory of evening. So close and familiar that it had become to me an inner temple resonating with a high song of lamentation and celebration. One night under a full moon, in the murmur of the waves, I heard the voice with the Oxford accent whispering in the ear of the young man of fifteen whom I still was: "You see, our dear Keats was right. The earth really is a place of initiation where one is transmuted into a soul. Having become souls, we find one another again, henceforth no distance can separate us!" Thus an incredible complicity was born between Shelley and me that, far from closing my life, gave it an unsuspected opening. I entered resolutely into another "realm."

⟿⟝

Allow me to relate another very recent and even more personal event. A few days ago I was in the midst of preparing this meditation when I received mail from the United States sent by the French-Chinese cellist Cécilia Tsan and conveyed by a friend who is attending our sessions. Cécilia Tsan expressed the wish to hear me talk about her father, knowing no doubt that I am the only one left now of those who knew him. This request suddenly took me back more than sixty years, to the early 1950s—a time so distant it seems to me to belong to a previous life.

I was then a young man full of torment and anguish because of my exile and my inability to get along in practical day-to-day life. Cécilia Tsan's father was a young man like me, just as unfit to face everyday life, but he had the good fortune to be married and already the father of a daughter. And above all, unlike me, he had no doubts about his vocation: a composer. Coming from the Shanghai conservatory, Guo-ling—a first name that means "Soul of the country"—numbered among the most promising of his generation. Aided by his charming wife, he came to France to perfect his art. I used to hear it said about him that he lived and breathed music, and although I don't know why, I compared him instinctively to Georges Bizet. Perhaps because of his extraordinary sense of rhythm and melody. I remember that it was while listening to one of his pieces, sustained by an entrancing rhythm, that I learned from him one of my first musical terms in French: *basse continue,* or continuo. Later, borrowing the idea from Jacques de Bourbon-Busset, I would use this notion of a continuo, as I said earlier, to define the soul of each being. Tsan lived in the suburbs and he got around on a bicycle. One night he did not come home. Having run into a tree in the dark, he was killed instantly, leaving behind a gaping silence, a stunned, broken song. Cécilia was only fourteen years old. I can imagine the difficult road that her mother, already poor, had to travel, all the pain and hardship of raising two daughters by herself.

I had never had contact with Cécilia before she wrote to me a few days ago. I had only had the opportunity to hear some of her marvelous interpretations on France Musique in the 1980s or '90s. And I had exclaimed to myself at that time, "Ah, the soul of her father passed into her!" When I received her unexpected letter, moved by her writing, as vibrant as her bow, I sent her the following poem:

Carnal soul, that continuo in each of us
When the touch of another makes it
Vibrate, resonate

Slowly then rises
Awakened then filled with wonder
Awakening then enchanting
The song of early childhood
Once resounding then forgotten
Long buried then remembered
Singing the psalms of the present in its
    fullness
Where the opened lily finally rejoins the star . . .

Isn't Being exactly this music
That since the beginning
Seeks to make itself heard
That waits
Each moment of each day
And each day of an entire life
For the hand to know finally to touch the
    lyre?

Moved in turn by my poem that she immediately learned by heart, Cécilia proposed passing it on to her friend the composer Éric Tanguy with the idea of having him write a score for it. And she added, "The piece could be called 'The Lily and the Lyre,' what do you think?" A very good title indeed. The phonic link between the two words calls up the link that exists between the lily and the lyre themselves. To me, it suggests the process of transformation and fusion that inevitably takes place between the fragile "perishable" lily and the eternal song of the lyre. It immediately inspired this thought in me: one day the lily opens into the lyre.

What I have just related gives me the distinct sensation of a soul-to-soul transmission, the singular conviction that somewhere something is finally fulfilled. And that the metamorphosis may already be beginning.

⌒ ◦ ⌒

I would now like to attest to a personal feeling I have experienced many times. Given my age, I've often been at the death bed of loved ones. These are individuals whose voices, looks, sensibilities, passions, shudders and groans, laughter and tears I've known intimately. Each time I've been struck by the discrepancy that exists between the unique being of the person and the lifeless body lying there before my eyes. Undeniably that body, now suddenly still, belonged to someone dear to me, a friend, yet I knew that being was not reduced to *that,* but already unbelievably freed, unified, elsewhere. That being was already present in some other way, and in some other way more present. I thought of Cocteau then who was struck with a sudden intuition at Giraudoux's solemn funeral procession and said to his friends, "But he's not there, let's go!" I also thought of Camus' sudden death, which had been a great shock for everyone. Through our reading, many of us were very familiar with this being of sharp intelligence and passionate temperament, driven by a fierce desire to live and a burning quest for justice and solidarity. Through accounts and images, the press went out of its way to show us what Camus had become: a mass of blood-streaked flesh and broken bones. I remember that a feeling of revolt—a word dear to Camus—swelled up in me: What? All his human dignity and nobility of mind could be reduced, in a second, to this pile of debris? Talk about the absurd—another theme dear to Camus—that would truly have been the word for this. Had the circumstances not been tragic, it would have been grotesque, even comic. But no, beyond the comedy or tragedy of our precariousness, well beyond, lies the high fact of being, the sacred fact of being. Nothing can change the fact that this man, this soul, existed. Nor can anything erase what constituted his uniqueness. Let us remember the words of Vladimir Jankélévitch: "If life is fleeting, the fact of having lived a fleeting life is an eternal fact."

But Camus, like everyone human who dies, nevertheless remains a mystery. Basically, what is he? What did he become? Why was he there, offering that singular face, bearing that particular name? Could his mind have stirred for nothing? His heart beat for nothing? We can ask these questions regarding ourselves, and we find ourselves once again up against the wall of that ultimate interrogation: where do we come from, who are we, where are we going? It is a wall that nonetheless sends back certain echoes. Because there is at least one thing we know: we come from the universe and the universe is very peacefully, very incredibly there, whatever happens to us individually. As for the rest, only God knows . . .

God? Ah, see how, as if by mistake, this word slips out! Moreover, is it simply a word or a proper name? In any case, it is at least a much debated term that encounters support from some and rejection from others. I rarely utter it, at least never lightly; I may even refrain from using it at all. But in this case, we would honestly have to invent another word to name what happened, what imposed those laws that function with such astounding, immediately apparent precision and sophistication and that endure over time. We would not be satisfied with a vision of the universe that supposedly made itself, all by itself, completely unconscious from start to finish, and that was supposedly capable of engendering conscious but transient beings like us who, in the space of a few seconds within eternity, could see and know it. For the idea of God to approach acceptability for the majority of us, let us try to begin with the minimum, by defining God as that by which the universe and life came about, that by which the progress of the Way is ensured.

In that last sentence, can we replace the pronoun "that" with "the One," that is to say, substitute for the idea of a principle that of a Being? We are thinking here of a personal God, because the immense adventure of life ends not in a collection of anonymous entities, but in each flower, each insect, each of us who have become individuals, composed of a body, mind, and soul; God can appear as no less. We inevitably seek to establish a being-to-Being relationship with the On High, a perfectly legitimate quest because what relationship could we have with a neutral, anonymous principle? Although described as nonreligious, Chinese thought does not reject such a relationship. Chinese thought affirms that within the Way resides the *shen,* the "divine," which provides the *shen-ch'i,* the "divine breath," or the *shen-ming,* the "divine spirit." These can be perceived as an intimate presence with which one is able to enter into relationship or dialogue. Moreover, the great Chuang Tzu evokes *Tso-wu-che,* "the One who made all things," four times in his work.

Does envisioning God diminish us? On the contrary, by integrating us into the progress of the Way, it can only enlarge us. That is what Rilke understood when he wrote, "There is in me, finally, an absolutely indescribable manner of and passion for experiencing God. . . . Throughout my life, it was for me only a matter of discovering and confirming that place in my heart that made me able to worship in all the temples considered to be the greatest on earth."*

We need to name God because we are situated resolutely in the order of life and we are meditating on our condition's limit, death. We need to have a dialogue with God, we need to ask God about the possible ways out. Is it too pretentious to present ourselves as God's interlocutors, even supposing that He may have created us for that? Here, the voices of those who remind us of the lost and isolated post-Copernican world make themselves heard. We recall the terror that seized the West when Copernicus discovered that Earth was not the center of the universe, that it was not God's favorite, that it was only a bit of the solar system. That terror increased when we learned that this system itself was only a tiny bit of an immense galaxy, which itself was only a nearly negligible bit of a whole beyond measure, composed of billions of other galaxies. Even today, when we truly fathom this situation, how can we not be dumbfounded? Nevertheless, when our amazement passes, we may wonder, "The Earth isn't at the center? In that case, where is the center?" For those informed by the vision of the Tao, whose movement is circular and in which everything is linked and holds together, the universe can be in continual expansion. It is sustained by Breath that circulates and does not falter. If such a vision is valid, all points rejoin

---

*Lou Albert-Lasard, *Une image de Rilke* [An Image of Rilke] (Paris, France: Mercure de France, 1953).

the All. Wherever an eye opens or a heart beats, the center is there.

Once again, we have no doubt that we are party to an immense adventure: Life. But honestly, do we know exactly what role we have in that cosmic adventure? Might we not be actors in a play, its stakes and outcome unknown to us? Completely unknown to us? Certainly not completely. About the mystery of life, we know a bit! Each of us bears within ourselves what humanity bears within itself. That is, all the extreme conditions of life, Heaven as well as hell, the heights as well as the depths, soaring toward the most elevated spheres and sinking to the most debased cruelty, moments of divine bliss and of atrocious suffering caused by radical evil. In humanity all frustrated aspirations and unmet desires open a gaping infinity that only eternity can fill. Our truth does not lie in the leveling and obliteration, but in the transmutation and transfiguration. We will only know true joy by accepting the pain and losses that overwhelm us; we will only know true peace when we embrace the bodies broken by suffering and torment. True life comes at this price.

At the heart of humanity, admirable figures have arisen who offer us light and consolation. They constitute human grandeur and draw us continually toward the heights. One day one arose among us, he strove toward absolute life, he took upon himself all the suffering of the world by giving his life, so that even the most humiliated, the most tortured can, in their utter darkness, identify with him and find comfort in him. If he did so, it was not to delight in suffering; he let himself be nailed on the cross to show the world that absolute love is possible, a love "as strong as death," and even stronger than death, capable of saying to its own executioners,

"Forgive them for they know not what they do." These words addressed to God are addressed to us as well, calling upon us to participate in divine forgiveness, to unite human becoming with divine becoming, and the uniqueness of each being with the uniqueness of Being itself. The one who speaks thus makes life's dark tunnel emerge into the Open. With him, death is no longer simply the proof of absolute life but also the proof of absolute love. With him, death changes in nature and dimension: it becomes the opening through which the infinite breath of transfiguration passes.

Yes, with him, death was transformed into true birth. And that took place on our Earth at a crucial moment in human history. Nobody had gone so far. Whatever our individual convictions, we can acknowledge this Christian event as one of the highest that has come to alter our consciousness.

Even among atheists and agnostics, many agree on this point. But God? What can we say about him? What can we say to him? If it is a matter of speaking *of him*, how to proceed, recognizing the vanity of any words before so vast a subject? And if it is a matter of speaking *to him*, how to circumvent our immediate reproaches: Why did you create such a rotten world? Why have you tolerated the ravages of evil? Why do you remain so silent before the scandal of innocent suffering? Why this passivity that has all the appearances of indifference? . . . The questions rush out and we receive no response. God does indeed remain silent. Perhaps he has to.

Here I propose that we attempt the same effort we tried during the first meditation: reverse our position, turn our perspective around. Instead of always positioning ourselves before the Creator, to come begging or in revolt, let us situate ourselves on the side of Creation and imagine what is possible. What strange, if not sacrilegious, audacity! But we are driven to this reversal, which could help us to see a little more clearly, to understand as the writer Teilhard de Chardin did that "to create is no small matter for the All Powerful, not a game. It is an adventure, a dangerous undertaking, a battle in which he engages fully."

Regarding the advent of life, right from the beginning the Creator must have found himself facing a dilemma. Just like us, he must have wanted a perfect world. For that to be so, he had only to create a group of perfectly obedient beings, like robots. He would raise his baton, all would get up; he would lower his baton, all would lie down. Then we are no longer in the order of life, and no joy can be drawn from it. For beings to achieve consciousness, to the point of being capable of knowing the created universe, they must be endowed with intelligence and freedom, conditions even more necessary if the Creation is to be animated by the principle of love.

Almost immediately a problem arises that will transform the process of life into drama: the problem of radical evil, as we saw in the last meditation. As a being endowed with intelligence and freedom, man, when he is moved by the desire for possession or domination, is capable of corrupting everything, causing incredible suffering, and threatening to destroy the order of life itself. In view of this situation, couldn't God intervene from time to time, easing things by means of salves and band-aids, correcting them with the slap of a ruler or night stick? No, of course not. If God is the one who ensures the progress of the Way, he cannot be capricious. True Creation is a total Gift, without reserve; it cannot proceed by small, improvised additions. The Confucian text *The Doctrine of the Mean* states: "The way of Heaven is constant and reliable; it neither alters nor fails. That is how the human way knows its path."

From this perspective, the development of life becomes an immense adventure, replete with remarkable advances as well as unforeseeable dangers, just as much an adventure for humans as for God. More accurately, we should say the human adventure becomes exactly God's adventure: if humans fail, it would be a failure for him. This God through whom life came about, through whom the progress of the Way is ensured, is not content with setting history in motion with an initial snap of the fingers, as Pascal described Descartes' God. No, he is the future God who will never stop becoming, as Moses heard from his mouth: "I will be what I will be." The human future is part of his adventure, thus it is he himself becoming.

Let us be clear that the future God is simultaneously the God of recollection. Because the true future is the metamorphosis of all past experience. Moreover that is how what has happened and what will happen form an eternal present. Forgetting nothing, God will accompany all, will gather all, to finally transform all. That is what Proust, for example, writing *Remembrance of Things Past,* understood in his totally human way. At the end of his book and his life, he said with regard to the death of Bergotte: "Dead forever? Who can say? . . . everything is arranged in this life as though we entered it carrying a burden of obligations contracted in a former life; there is no reason inherent in the conditions of life on this earth that can make us consider ourselves obliged to do good, to be kind and thoughtful, even to be polite, nor for an atheist artist to consider himself obliged to begin over again a score of times a piece of work the admiration aroused by which will matter little to his worm-eaten body, like the patch of yellow wall painted with so much skill and refinement by the artist destined to be forever unknown and barely identified under the name Vermeer. All these obligations, which have no sanction in our present life, seem to belong to a different world, a world based on kindness, scrupulousness, self-sacrifice, a world entirely different from this one and which we leave in order to be born on this earth, before perhaps returning there to live once again beneath the sway of those unknown laws which we obeyed because we bore their precepts in our hearts, not knowing whose hand had traced them there."*

Whatever his anxiety and concern for us, the God of recollection, infinitely present, still maintains silence. Until there is a new order, he must leave the universe in transformation to follow the dynamic of its course until the end. A transfiguration would only be able to take place beginning from that which is given. In this sense, we can say that God, obliged to silence, is, in his way, "fragile." That is why in the depths of the abyss opened by radical evil, we other humans hear the voice of Etty Hillesum, a frail voice, but so clear, so resolute: "These are times of terror, my God. Tonight for the first time I stayed awake in the dark, my eyes burning, images of human suffering parading endlessly before me. I am going to promise you one thing, my God, oh, a trifle: I will not let myself weigh down the present day with those fears that the future inspires in me; but that requires some training. . . . My God, I am going to help you not to extinguish yourself in me, but I can guarantee nothing in advance. Nevertheless one thing appears to me more and more clearly: it is not you

*Marcel Proust, *Remembrance of Things Past,* vol. 3, *The Captive,* trans. C. K. Scott Moncrieff (New York: Random House, 1981).

who can help us, but we who can help you, and in so doing, we help ourselves."*

These words echo the famous poem by Rilke, of whom Etty was a passionate reader:

> *What will you do, God, if I die?*
> *I am your pitcher, if I break?*
> *I am your drink, if I am altered?*
> *I am your robe and your mission,*
> *With me absent, you would lose all*
> *meaning.*†

A singular, shared adventure, the only one that actually has value; otherwise, let us repeat, all the splendor of the universe would be in vain. Yes, there is only one adventure that for all eternity had to happen and that for all eternity has to continue. But in what manner? Through an indefinite extension of the same order? Like Rimbaud, all of us, at some moment or another in our lives, have exclaimed to ourselves: "True life is absent!" Because of all our failures, God must have let out this cry as well. True life is the irrepressible desire for life, the infinite surge toward life, the inexhaustible nostalgia for total life. The need to transmute the process of life into the superior order of true life will assert itself as an obvious fact. Weighed down with all the experience of life here and now, we want this but cannot have it. If the one who created the universe and life wants this, he can have it. On this subject let us recall what Lao Tzu affirms in the *Tao Te*

---

*Une vie bouleversée [A Life Turned Upside Down] (Paris, France: Seuil, 1985).

†Rilke, *The Book of Hours.*

Ching: "No going out without coming back," meaning that the power capable of engendering has the capacity to gather everything in.

How would he set about it? Would he need to create a new generation of unknown beings unfamiliar with both suffering and death, who would view life not as an unbelievable gift but as a simple given and their due? We have seen how unproductive such a false reality is in our first meditation. For the order of true life to emerge, God will need nothing less than the whole of human experience on this Earth. He will need all those who went through life here below, who went through death and bear within all the hunger and thirst, all the suffering and failings, all the endless surges toward the true life. Through all the trials of unfulfilled love, their souls have absorbed the gifts of the body and the mind. Having become souls, they are finally free and capable of living the true life. Once again the trustworthy intuition of the poet resounds: "The earth is a valley where souls grow."

Yes, there is only one adventure, and if each of us has only one life, all Life is one. To have been is an eternal fact, because it partakes of the sublime promise: "I will be what I will be."

FIFTH MEDITATION

The trees of infinite sadness
The clouds of infinite joy
Sometimes offer some sign of life
At the edge of vast summer.

The skylarks pass through
Without grasping any of their words,
One spring alone will retain them
To offer a drink to the dead.

Some poems, altered or revised here, appear in the following collections: *Cantos toscans* [Tuscan Cantos] (Nice, France: Unes, 1999); *Qui dira notre nuit* [Who Will Speak Our Night] (Paris, France: Arfuyen, 2003); *Le Livre du Vide médian* [The Book of the Median Void] (Paris, France: Albin Michel, 2004, new edition 2009).

But that which was lived
will be dreamed,
And that which was dreamed
relived.

We will not have too long a night

To burn the branches that fell
without our knowing it,
To gather in the lasting scent
of smoke.

Let that which we believed lost come back
To us from the other realm, let them come
     back,
Those who, in going away, said nothing,
Let their mute cry be our daily bread,
Let what is bitter and torn come back
     whole:
Because bite and remorse are of a piece,

Gentleness and pain lean on one another.

Follow the fish, follow the bird.
If you envy their glide, follow them
To the end. Follow their flight, follow
Their dive, until you become
Nothing. Nothing more than the blue from
        which
This ardent transformation one day surged,

The desire itself to swim, to fly.

Death cannot be our outcome,
Because greater than we are
Is our desire, which rejoins
That of the Beginning,
The desire to Live.

Death cannot be our outcome,
But it makes everything here unique:
This dew that opens today's blossoms,
This sun that transforms the landscape,
This lightning when eyes meet,
And the blaze of a late autumn,
This perfume that overwhelms then
    fades, elusive,
These whispers that revive the native
    tongue,
These hours radiant with cheers, with
    hallelujahs,
These hours pervaded with silence, with
    absence,

This thirst that will never be quenched,
And hunger that has no end but infinity . . .

Faithful companion, death compels us
To burrow endlessly into ourselves
To harbor dream and memory there,
To hollow forever within ourselves
The tunnel leading to open air.

It cannot be our outcome.
Setting the limit,
It signifies to us the most
Extreme demand of Life,
Which gives, uplifts,
Overflows and surpasses.

Descend to the humus where tears and dew
Mix, spilled blood and inviolate spring,
Where tortured bodies again find soft clay,
Humus ready to receive fears and pains,
So that everything comes to an end and
      nevertheless nothing is lost.

Descend to the humus where the promise of
Original breath lies hidden. Single place of
Transmutation where fears and pains
Uncover peace and quiet. Thus decay and
      nourishment
Are joined, form just one word and seed.
Place of choice: the way of death leads to
      nothingness,
The desire for life leads to life. Yes, the
      miracle takes place
So that everything comes to an end and
      nevertheless every end can be a birth.

Descend to the humus, consent
To be humus itself, unite your own suffering

With the suffering of the world, unite
The killed voices with the song of the
*   bird, the frost-covered bones with the*
*   snowdrop's racket!*

When the angel makes a sign,
We will know that the Double Realm is
    reunited,
The great wind crossing the whole surface
Of the earth from end to end,
These words finally rejoining the other side.

That which has yet to live and that which
    has lived,
That which tends toward joy and that
    which is suffering
Conjugate into a present of grief and
    expectation,
Time stopped
Is nothing more than latent transformation.

The water in the river evaporates into
    cloud, falls again
As rain, renourishes, invisible,
The current of the eternal return,

Wounded faces, strangled voices come back
to us,
Transfigured by breath and blood.

The unformulated and the unaccomplished
mixing
With the unexpected and the unhoped for,
Flowing together here, they become the
moment's fountain
That henceforth recaptures everything, lets
everything rise
Inexhaustibly springing forth.

When the angel makes a sign,
We will know that what is born of us
Will now never cease to come to pass,
Ahead of us, without our knowing it,
To overtake us suddenly, and save us.

Sometimes the absent ones are there
More intensely there
Mixing with human talk
Human laughter
That depth of gravity
That they alone
Can retain
That they alone
Can dispel
Too intensely there
They keep silent still.

⊘

Do not forget those in the depths of the
   abyss,
Without fire, lamp, consoling cheek,
Helping hand . . . Do not forget them,
Because they remember flashes of
   childhood,
Bursts of youth—life echoing in
Fountains, in the driving wind—where
   will they go

If you forget them, you, God of memory?

You, forever springing forth

Spreading wave after wave
Your breath casting shade
For all creation that flows

Sometimes you greet
The man nailed fast
Over there

The man teaching and bleeding
Who will never cease
Following your example
Giving back life

To dead wood

Speak to us
So that nothing more be lost,
Neither the lightning embracing the pines,
Nor the warm clay with its crickets.

Hear us
So that our voices mixed with your own,
Pouring forth the glory of a brief summer,
Finally establish the realm.

Since all of life is linked,
We will submit
To the tide that carries away the moon,
To the moon that brings back the tide,
To the dead without whom we would not be,
To the survivors without whom we would not be,
To the unheard calls that diminish,
To the mute cries that continue,
To the looks frozen by fear
At the end of which a child's song returns,
To what returns and goes away no more,
To what returns and fades into the dark,
To each star lost in the night,
To each tear dried in the night,
To each night of a life,
To each minute
Of a single night
When all that is linked
Is reunited,
To life free of forgetting,
To death abolished.

Here we are in the abyss,
You remain the enigma.

Say a single word,
And we will be saved,

Still you remain mute,
To the very end seem deaf.

Our hearts are too hardened,
Within us, fathomless horror.

Would a glimmer of gentleness
Come from us?

And if we say one word,
You will be saved.

Still we remain mute,
To the very end remain deaf.

Here you are in the abyss,
We are the enigma.

Thus the time has come, Lord
To take a hard look at life
According to you, not according to us.
Accompany us to the end
So that all our wealth be saved.
But you, we have lost you.

Will you come on time, Lord?

Night, mother of lights,
Light is in her breast.

Already blood, already milk,
Already torn flesh,

Already way of tenderness,
Already way of sorrow,

Already ready to die,
But always reborn,

Already final leap,
But always

first run.

Nevertheless it still remains to us to
    celebrate as you do
To celebrate what, having sprung up among
    us, still reaches toward open life
What, from wounded flesh, cries remember
What, from spilled blood, cries justice
The only way truly open to us still to honor
    the suffering and the dead.

Each of us is finite
The infinite is what, having arisen among
    us, makes up the unexpected and the
    unhoped-for
To celebrate the beyond of desire, the beyond
    of self
Is the only way truly open to us still to keep
    the initial promise
To celebrate the fruit, and even more than
    the fruit, its infinite flavor

To celebrate the word, and even more than
   the word, its infinite echo.
To celebrate the dawn of reinvented names

To celebrate the dusk of eyes that meet
To celebrate the night of the emaciated faces
Of the dying who no longer hope for
   anything but who await us all
Within us the never-to-be-lost
That we try to return as an offering
The only way open where life will offer itself
   endlessly with open palms.

When the oriole's song suddenly falls silent,
Space is filled with things that die.
The long cascade of a waterfall
Opens the rocks at its depths;
The valley is listening and hears the echo
Of heartbeats immemorial.

This path that we crossed
one night
Child of my gaze
you will extend
Beyond the forest
a pond may be sleeping
Or a beach wandering
according to the waves

This starry path
you will extend
Despite wind and dew
child of my memory
From this side autumn
buried its secret
In you time flies mad
with cries of wild geese

Lerici Elegy
To Shelley

*Here we are finally reunited. Because never
Have I forgotten your distant call
Hurled over the unleashed waves,
Call heard one day in the deepest depths
Of a Chinese valley . . . Oh, miracle
Of fate! I find myself here, in this place
Of your farewells, your voice suddenly
    within earshot
Of the heart, of the body: the sun
Burning still, or soft whispers, calmed.
Yes, here we are reunited, me having
    traversed
The passes of space and the cycles of time,
You, at the end of wandering, having left
Your singular imprint here. White presence
Of this temple of song, at the base of hills
Overlooking the sea. Immutable whiteness
Nonetheless transmuting: noble diadem*

In the fire of the sunset, giant star
At the heart of the vast stellar night.

⌒◦⌒

Night, night, darkness without bounds.
    What does it know
Of the mystery of light? What does it foresee
For the sun and the planet Earth? And you,
What have you seen of it, you, the chosen
        bard,
Our guide for this insane adventure?
Dust amid dust, vanity
Of vanities? Vain, the abysses over which
We have leaned? Vain, the peaks
Toward which we have strived? Vain,
Our defiance in the face of tyranny, our horror
Before human cruelty? Vain themselves,
These moments of ecstasy that we have stolen
From the rhythmic circulating breath? Is
        there
A homeland other than our earthly habitat?
Another hell besides our Earth?

⌒◦⌒

Oh you who feel, tell us what you know.
Tell us to what degree of atrocity
Man is able to stoop. To what

Bottomlessness? As forgetting is no longer
    enough,
Could even death itself bring it to an end?
You who lived through quest after quest,
    and perished
In the waves' fury, those high waves
That are only of this world without equal,
Tell us what you have learned about its fate.

⟶⟵

Isolated place of damnation within an
    infinite
Cosmos? Place of endless experimentation
For the genius of evil? Our Earth, dark
    star!
What could have haunted your imagination
Two centuries ago? Lions' pit where living
    flesh,
prompted by cheers, let itself be torn
To shreds; torture chamber and public
    burning
Where living flesh, cries gone silent, was
    consumed
Under red hot iron or flame; battlefield
Where, offering itself to knife blades, the
    same flesh
Was slashed to the bone, then left

To the crows. In constant progress,
    humanity
Progresses certainly, too often into horror!
Of this we can testify after you:
Pregnant women disemboweled seeing their
    babies
Hurled into the air, men forced to dig
The pits where they will be buried alive,
    joining
The countless victims of modern monsters,
Cluster bombs, neutron bombs . . . always
    more superior,
Chemical weapons, biological weapons . . .
    always more subtle,
Actual cattle trucks to crush the face of
    humanity,
Factories of death to reduce bodies and souls
    to ashes.
Dust amid dust, vanity
Of vanities? Are we still allowed to forget?
Can death still serve as our way out?
We are sons of the damned, we are
Sons of the martyrs! Their thirst, their
    hunger
Is ours. Their stifled sobs
Are ours. We owe it to them to breathe in

The spring, to breathe out the eternal
    summer,
We owe it to them to live the life of the
    present,
To search again for the possibilities once
    buried there.

⟶⟵

Let us pose the endless chain of questions:
How can man, eaten away by radical evil, evil
That comes from his own ingenuity that
    nothing can stop,
Claim, without shame, to be the measure
Of all things? Isn't he rather in a position
To destroy the order of Life itself?
Isn't it time for him to become more
    obliging again,
More in accord with his first calling, and
    that calling
More in accord with the whole universe,
Whose advent, as the Ancients saw,
Was all glory? Isn't it time for him to
    celebrate
Once again the unbelievable gift of the Gift?
If the Promethean fire still remains alive,
The Christian way too remains open.

⌒⌒

Yes, to rediscover the good that was lost,
To look hard at naked truth, and in doing so
Envision sure beauty. Because you were
　　　Ariel,
You were Skylark. Fallen angel or native
　　　daemon,
Were you nostalgia? Were you prophecy?
Beyond the man who reasons, weren't you
Man who resonates to unheard-of song?
More than thief of fire, you were bearer
Of sparks that produced illumination.
Wearing a miner's headlamp, you became
Tracker of the magic spells of this world:
Starry vault, sparkling fields of azaleas,
Feminine grace embracing curves of hills,
Lake water transformed into cloud vapor,
And children's laughter into lovers' smiles,
Passionate pursuit of too distant a face,
Thirsty whispers sealed by a kiss . . .
Then, to the extent that you penetrated
　　　grief,
Other beauties sometimes struck you:
Noble and worthy gaze before the
　　　implacable sword,
Tortured body that tender hands revive.

⌒⌒

Strange promise of this anonymous earth!
You, free spirit, wandering from place to
    place,
One day you landed at this point on the globe,
The heights of a mountain in the Apennines.
Stretching before your eyes to the distant
    horizon,
The Mediterranean cradle-grave so long
    dreamed of.
Contemplating it with your whole soul wide
    awake,
There you discerned the sleeping gods, and
    you exulted:
"Blessed be the present hour, this ground;
Blessed be our body through which feeling
    passes.
Space of a lightning flash—but in what lost
    corner
Within the staggering sidereal immensity?
Lightning flash of this small heart that beats
    there,
On this afternoon of a summer solstice . . .
Blessed be the miracle that makes that be.
That is! This improbable and undeniable
    Life,

Once for all—thus for always—
Offered. In this place of origin, the light
Renews its advent. From sepia shadow
Radiates golden yellow and sapphire blue.
    Then
Rising from the humus, the scents of lichen
And grass, softening the hot rocks
Of barely extinguished lava. Then humming,
Droning, the latent desires spread out.
All the living beings that chance brings
        together—each unique
Presence coming to pass—prove necessary
To the beauty of this moment. Oh
        memorable marriage
Of twisting roots and hovering mist,
Of intermittent orioles and continuous
        waterfall!
—What is there, invisible, lending an ear,
        offering itself
To the eye, to the encounter of the
        incarnate?—Here, here,
The floral scent on the hives of bees that
        throng
The leaps of a doe, the sea breeze on the wings
Of elves that the pines carry to the clouds . . . "

⌒⌒

Over there, very low, a hidden bay opens
Her arms like a lover in a gesture of
*   invitation.*
You hear the voice of the waves that speaks
*   to you*
Most intimately: "Lost soul, allow yourself
A rest, be the guest here, let your sojourn
Take place here. Because it is good for your
*   dreams,*
If your heart is worthy of it, that all that
Was done." Obedient, you rise and go down
Toward the bay, toward your supreme
*   sojourn*
Which will forever be conjugated in the
*   present.*
Ah, let the dawn come, and the sea, dazzled,
In abeyance; you dive in, carried
By the brightness of the morning of the
*   world.*
Let the dusk come, and the sea, conquered,
In offering; you dive in, delivered
To the brilliance of all the worlds beyond.
Woman in love becomes the sea, when
*   drawn*
By the full moon; rocked by the frail
*   barque,*

Your words ravish the enamored souls.
Divine sojourn? Human sojourn! Taking part
In the laughter and tears of the nearby
    fishermen,
Under the generous sun, you cannot forget
All the damned of your old country,
Their damp alleys, their moldy prisons . . .
How to deny, nevertheless, that beauty has
    a place?
Nothing more can happen to repudiate its
    splendor.
Its passion lives on; we ourselves change,
Dust amid dust, vanity
Of vanities? Then where does this
    unappeasable emotion
Come from? This piercing trepidation?
Lost within the immensity, space of a
    lightning flash,
This speck of dust—by what magic—become
    man
Saw, heard, was moved, was transformed
In language, in exchange, in long songs
Of revolt, of torment, of praise?
To sing, that's it! To sing, isn't this
To resonate? With what else except Being?
To sing, to truly sing, is to raise oneself

To the ceaseless call of Being, it is to be!
Could it be by chance that we are the
    beating heart,
The wakened eye of this cosmos?
Carried by the Breath, always higher,
    always clearer,
Unaware of limits, our response to the call,
Laden with so many unfulfilled desires,
Goes to the furthest bounds of the eternal.

⌒◦⌒

Divine sojourn? Human sojourn! Oh yes,
True beauty, being affirmed glory,
Will never cease to shine
And its flight will never falter. Only we,
Unrepentant seekers that we are, will
    disappear.
You, in full bliss, you are not without vision:
If the sea grants benevolence to the ground
That knows how to welcome it in all humility,
Elsewhere it does not in the least renounce
Its tempestuous powers. It is up to man
To learn the fair measure, up to him
To consent to the scarce, to the brief, to the
    unique.
The way of grief leads to the inner voice,
The pincers of regret to the cries of the entrails.

Having once been the cause of an early death,
And coming from mourning your Friend, you
    understood
That in you the song of Orpheus was achieved.
Despite the violence of the final wrenching,
Despite the shudders of horror at the moment
Of the ordeal, to yield suddenly to death
Seemed to you, in the end, fair.

⌒

"Here I am stretched out on the pyre, limbs
    numb,
Hair soaked, in the scent of the sand
And the seaweed. Oh dearest ones who
    surround me,
Do not be at all afraid, do not be grieved,
Do not let yourselves drown anymore in tears!
Abandon this body now devoured
By the fire. Aren't the desires that we bear
Greater than us? So great
That they rejoin the original Desire through
    which
There was light. Thus let my flame
Rise and rent the night, which, in
    welcoming,
Opens the Milky Way
of Transfiguration."

Passing through, leave in this place
Neither the treasures of your body
Nor the gifts of your mind
But a few footprints

So that one day the great wind
Is initiated into your rhythm,
Into your silence, into your cry,
And at last determines your way.

BOOKS OF RELATED INTEREST

The Way of Beauty
Five Meditations for Spiritual Transformation
by François Cheng

The Spirituality of Age
A Seeker's Guide to Growing Older
by Robert L. Weber, Ph.D. and Carol Orsborn, Ph.D.

Nine Designs for Inner Peace
The Ultimate Guide to Meditating with Color, Shape, and Sound
by Sarah Tomlinson

Breathing through the Whole Body
The Buddha's Instructions on Integrating Mind, Body, and Breath
by Will Johnson

Fusion of the Five Elements
Meditations for Transforming Negative Emotions
by Mantak Chia

Living in the Tao
The Effortless Path of Self-Discovery
by Mantak Chia and William U. Wei

The Practice of Tibetan Meditation
Exercises, Visualizations, and Mantras for Health and Well-being
by Dagsay Tulku Rinpoche

Meditations on the Peaks
Mountain Climbing as Metaphor for the Spiritual Quest
by Julius Evola

Inner Traditions • Bear & Company
P.O. Box 388
Rochester, VT 05767
1-800-246-8648
www.InnerTraditions.com

Or contact your local bookseller